To madeleine & Bill

A View from the Bucket

all the best!

Jean Fedekopp

Cover and inside photographs from the Young family albums.

Book design by Joe Blades/Maritimes Arts Projects Productions.

Printed and bound in Canada by Sentinel Printing

Canadian Cataloguing in Publication Data
Redekopp, Jean, 1938-

    A view from the bucket

    ISBN 0-921411-52-9

1. Redekopp, Jean, 1938-   2. Grand Lake Region (Queen's, N.B.) — Biography.   3. McNab's Island (N.S.) — Biography. I. Title.

FC2042.R42A3 1996   971.5'42   C96-950133-1
F1035.8.R42 1996

Maritimes Arts Projects Productions
Box 596   Ph   506 454·5127
Fredericton NB E3B 5A6   Fax 506 454·5127
Canada   E-mail jblades@nbnet.nb.ca

A View From the Bucket

Jean Redekopp

Fredericton · Canada

A View from the Bucket

If one could remember the sounds and smells from the moment they came into the world, most babies would remember the warmth of their mother's arms, the cosiness of their surroundings, the brightness of the room and probably many persons milling around with either stressful or happy expressions on their faces.

This atmosphere did not exist when I entered the world, for I was born in an old farmhouse with only my mother present and a sibling that had barely reached the age of two. Where that sibling was at that exact moment is hard to know, as there was no sitter, no father, no doctor or nurse present.

It was not an easy birth, and apparently a long hard labour, as the fires in both the kitchen and living room wood stoves had long since burned out, leaving a strong draft in the upstairs bedroom.

Temperatures in New Brunswick in late January are not kind or pleasant. The wind blew at a furious pace across Grand Lake, a few hundred feet behind our farmhouse for most of the winter months.

In 1938 we were not aware of any "warming trend" and coped with survival by filling the wood stoves around the clock and banking the outside of the house with fresh sawdust donated by a kindly neighbour a few miles down the road.

One thing Mother didn't have to contend with in those months was dust from the narrow dirt road that passed by our house.

Fred, as we called him as kids, was supposed to have gone to our only neighbour with a phone to call for a Mrs. Tower to come and tend my sister Betty, and to help Mom with the new baby. Fred, not being too dependable, had gone alright, left Betty behind on her own, but for some reason, did not return until everything was over and my mother was the tired and not too happy parent of another ten pound baby girl.

Mrs. Tower never did arrive because there was no way for her to arrive. Snow had accumulated to the point where only the rural mailman got through with tire chains for traction and then only when visibility allowed him to trespass on this narrow road with only the hydro poles to guide him.

These hydro poles were new with no wires connecting them as yet. The fact that they even existed was a great source of joy and anticipation of things to come, as those on this stretch of highway had always depended on oil lamps, ice boxes and battery operated radios. Our farmhouse was fairly up-to-date. We had a radio, two stoves, wooden storm windows and an outhouse not too far from the back door of the woodshed. The fact that our apple trees and one cherry tree had long since gone wild didn't seem to matter.

To bath this newborn required my mother to get out of her bed, get the kitchen stove fired up again, retreat to the hand-operated pump in the woodshed (another modern convenience), draw the water and place the galvanized washtub on the stove and wait patiently for some warmth in the kitchen as well as in the washtub. She had experience at this having gone through it two years previously with sibling number one, only the first time she performed this chore was in early June.

Having got through this delivery without suffering too much, life went back to a fairly smooth routine.

For some unknown reason, Fred wasn't too great around the house. Mother routinely tied Betty in the highchair and I was likely left in my crib or playpen while she trudged off to the barn to tend our one cow and the few chickens still to be taken care of. Being a "clean and neat" fanatic, she daily scoured out the cow stall (and probably scoured the cow as well), gave the chickens fresh straw and disposed of the used straw. It would be after dark when her chores were finished and she would pick her way through the snow back to the farmhouse where she'd find Fred waiting for a hot meal with the radio on, two babies howling and the fires ready for more wood.

Two more years passed. There was still no hydro, possibly having something to do with the fact that most able men had gone off to war.

Going off to war was discussed in our household but not much action was taken.

I didn't know enough to ask about money because I didn't know about such things at age two.

Doris' birth was about to take place, and fortunately, it was mid-September so Fred was sent off to use the only phone a half-mile down the road to call Mrs. Tower to come. She came two days after the baby was born, estimated it weighed at least thirteen pounds, and tried to tend to all our needs.

Fred must have enjoyed her cooking because I only remember her preparing his meals. Betty and I watched him devour the huge plates of fried potatoes, sausages, eggs, pancakes and chunks of homemade bread. He would use his fork as a spear to retrieve anything that was nearby. Mom would reprimand us for such behaviour but it was more fun to spear our food and get Fred encouraging us than it was to eat in a mannerly fashion.

Fred was turning into a real fun father. He allowed us to fill our mouths with water and squirt each other and him while Mom was at the barn. We could run in a big circle in our house if we opened up the "parlour" door and the door leading to an unused sun porch. We'd run with our mouths full of water and squirt each other with pretty good accuracy. One hazard of this activity was if you laughed, you choked. Since we knew the wet floors would be noticed when Mom got back from the barn chores, we would overdo the choking activity and be really in bad shape when Mom came in. That way we didn't get into trouble—Fred did!

Getting back to the room known as the parlour: it's purpose was to serve as a showplace for family members who might die and needed a quiet and peaceful place to be laid out for viewing. Since no one in our family was going to die, we figured the room might as well be used for horseplay. Normally the door was kept closed and there was no heat in there. It was very private and one could be in there for hours undetected unless a fight broke out.

This was a great room to take the stolen cookies or make cutouts from the Eaton's or Simpson's catalogues. Unfortunately, there were times when Mom would plant herself in the living room with the radio which was just on the other side of the parlour door and we'd be trapped in there. We'd wait a decent length of time, enjoy the peace and quiet before she'd leave her chair and go stick her head outside and call us. This gave us ample time to get our booty out of there and race upstairs to hide the contraband in our bedroom. There were times the parlour would get an infestation of ants and Mom would blame the poor fitting windows and warmer weather for this. By the time she'd discovered the ants, they'd cleaned up all the cookie crumbs and we stood there looking like the angels we were.

Cutting up the catalogues too soon had it's draw back as well. There were times when she wanted to order from the catalogue, only to find it shredded. The fate of the catalogues eventually was to be hung on the old coat hanger in the modern outhouse and used sparingly, as these catalogues were only printed twice a year and came through the mail as did any orders.

The paper in these things was not intended for the purpose to which it was put. Sharp corners were hazardous to our bottoms unless we took each individual page and crumpled it thoroughly, crunching it in both hands and really working it over. This activity usually took place while we were not too firmly planted on the adult-sized holes. Many times we'd need more than one page to do the job because, if the softening process went on too long, holes would appear and then it was discarded, unused.

Our outhouse was the only outhouse I ever used that didn't smell like an outhouse. It smelled of Mom's favourite disinfectant—Creolin. The less one breathed in there, the better it was for the lungs.

Being a modern building, we had wash tubs directly beneath the holes and a back-hinged flap that lifted up for easy access to the tubs. These were taken out periodically, probably spring and fall, loaded carefully onto the wheelbarrow and carted off to the lake, emptied into the lake, rinsed, disinfected of course, and returned to their proper position.

By now Betty had reached age five and I was three, so Mom figured Betty was old enough to take full responsibility for my well being and safety. We shared a bedroom as well as a bed and clothes. Doris remained in Mom and Fred's room in the crib. This room had heat because it was the only bedroom with a grate in the floor directly over the living room stovepipe.

That grate provided a direct source of heat on which Betty and I slept in the winter when our own room was too cold. We'd simply get out of our bed, trot across the hall and sprawl face down on the register. At least our faces would be hot, plus this grate had a second purpose: we could see and hear right down into the living room, listen to the radio, listen to Mom and Fred discuss our Christmas presents, and hear any conversations between them and any company that might come by. Besides, if you spit directly on the stovepipe, it was usually hot enough to really sizzle and foam. Sometimes if you really worked up a good mouthful, it would run off the stovepipe and land on the top of the stove. Unfortunately, when this happened, Mom would hear it and we'd have to boot it off to our own room, pretend to sleep and hope to get away with our little secret. Many a winter night she'd come upstairs at her

bedtime and find two kids asleep on the grate with its imprint
on our faces.

It was in the bedroom that I first became aware of time.

In the closet was a calendar and one day I discovered the
old calendar had disappeared and a new one was there in it's
spot. Of course I was disappointed, it had always been there for
as long as I could remember. Then I asked why this was done.
My mother explained that the year number had changed from
1942 to 1943 and proceeded to explain the whole senseless
system of keeping track of time.

The only good thing about this system was that my
birthday showed up on the very first page. So, I invented
''counting the days'' with a little help from my older sister.

It was somewhere in this period of time that Fred was sort of
''shoved off'' into the army. My mother finally convinced him
that if he didn't do something to earn some money we were
surely going to starve to death during this winter.

It was arranged with the neighbour with the coveted phone
to use his car (which was also the only car), a 1928 Model T
Ford with very yellow windows, to drive Fred to the railway
station some thirty miles away to catch the train to wherever he
was to go to receive his basic training.

This event was happening on a very cold, rainy day and,
my mother being a clean freak, had scrubbed the kitchen
linoleum with her usual heavy duty equipment and
disinfectants so, if Charlie should come in, the floor was
polished to a high gloss.

For some unknown reason the bucket of used water was
still in front of the kitchen stove. She got Betty and myself into
our heavy clothes and prepared the baby for this ''trip of a
lifetime.'' Fred didn't seem to know he was responsible for
emptying the bucket, so it remained right where Mom finished
her job.

Since I looked upon myself as a slow learner, I was
walking backwards in the kitchen in anticipation of Charlie's

arrival and managed to go backwards into this bucket of water. The first impulse was to scream and fake an injury or a scald. I'd think of some reason before Mom arrived from upstairs, toting the now well bundled baby.

This episode struck Fred as being terribly funny and he wasn't about to rescue me from the bucket. Well, Mom's screaming at him soon drowned out my screaming so there was a fight on and I innocently watched this from the bucket.

Once plucked from the bucket, I was stripped to the bare hide and prepared for the trip again in some clothes of Betty's that were still too big for me.

By this time, the baby was overheated and howling to the top of her lungs. Charlie arrived with his only daughter, who was roughly our age, but couldn't keep up with the antics of what now would be called a "dysfunctional family."

The trip was exciting because it was my first experience in a car, not to mention we had Charlie, Fred, Mom, Betty, Goldie (Charlie's daughter), myself and a baby all in one small car.

I believe we covered the distance in record-breaking time, deposited Fred on the platform, and headed home before the train actually arrived. This puzzled me as to why we would just leave him there alone, in the middle of nowhere, with no train in sight. What if that train never came? How would he get home or, worse still, in whose house would he live, as there didn't seem to be any houses in sight.

Once delivered back at our house, Charlie didn't come in, so all Mom's efforts to clean the kitchen linoleum were in vain.

The house seemed strangely quiet with Fred not there. Was Mom happy he was gone and she could get on with her cleaning, or was she already anticipating that first army cheque in the mail so she could order the winter supply of stove wood and phone in a big grocery order from Saint John and have it come to us via the train (if a train truly existed)?

Before too many weeks went by, sure enough, a load of
wood arrived. Mom got her yardstick out and measured it off
and decided she's been gypped on the cord she'd ordered. She
peeled off some money, and argument ensued, and the man
drove off yelling, "Order your wood from someone else, next
time."

These events were usually very exciting to me, since we
seldom saw a stranger, and for one to get so angry really got
our adrenaline going. So Betty and I decided to mimic him.
This did not set well with Mom, so we got our bottoms
smacked and sent to find a saw and an axe.

The wood was probably in four-foot lengths and the
firebox in the stove was definitely not that long. Mom
immediately set to work with the saw. The sawing seemed to
go on forever, day and night, until every last log looked like it
might fit into the stoves. Now came the chopping block. Betty
was given an axe and a few words of encouragement and
instruction, and her very own chopping block.

Now the chopping began, day and night, while the baby
was propped up in her carriage. I was busy carting the cut
wood into the woodshed.

It had to be stacked neatly, not just thrown into the one
section of woodshed that had no floor. This meant, even with
my arms full of wood, I had to be careful not to fall off the end
of the floor into the hole.

I honestly believe our house was warmer that winter than
any other winter. And, just as I'd imagined, a huge box of
groceries plus a few cartons of canned goods arrived via
Charlie. There were canned peaches, canned milk, canned
soups and a few other items that I had no intention of eating.
The interesting thing about all this was that our groceries came
in an aluminum lined box that had once held bulk tea. It was
soon discovered by Betty and myself that this aluminum had a
very distinct taste once peeled off the inside of the box and
sucked on. There was no talk at that time of aluminum causing
Alzheimer's disease!

Now that we had our own method of getting groceries, we were not so dependent upon the neighbours for surplus food. We were suddenly given canned milk which sure didn't taste like the warm, unpasteurized milk from our cow.

It was decided that our cow wasn't needed anymore and was to be sold. When we heard this, we decided that whoever was getting our cow, wasn't going to have any milk that might still be inside her.

Betty was pretty good at getting the milk out of her by now, so the cat and I would follow her into the pasture and wait patiently while she did her milking. Being short, I didn't need to kneel down to get a few good squirts right in the face, but most of it did get into my mouth. The cat had the right idea. She'd just jump in the general direction from where the milk was coming and get hers almost always in the mouth. I remember her thoroughly washing up after such strenuous exercise in getting her fair share of the warm milk. So, now that Betty was making sure the cow would have no milk for her new owner, Mom was finding that the cow seemed to be "going dry" and it was good that she had a buyer before she went completely dry.

I believe the few chickens we had were probably killed off, one by one, and eaten. We were never told this, but by now we could count and we were coming up short on chickens.

By now Betty and I were pretty independent; both of us could swim. We had easy access to the lake—just stroll down the extension of our driveway and we could walk or jump off the pier. We didn't know about bathing suits so we were usually just in our underwear. This activity cut way down on Mom having to prepare baths for us between mid-May and early October.

Even though our kitchen window faced down the driveway to the lake, Mom apparently was not aware that I could do a pretty good dog-paddle in eighteen feet of water. And being only four years old, I innocently one day invited her to watch this accomplishment. She was astounded that I would even think of jumping off the pier with only Betty there in case I got into trouble. She, herself, couldn't swim and to my knowledge, had never even been in the lake. So a rope was got from the barn and tied securely about my waist and I led her down the driveway like a dog leading his master with a leash. She gave me about fifteen feet of rope, stood well back from the edge of the pier, and said, ''Let's see you do it, then.''

So off I went into the water. Betty was there in case I needed her. And with rope tangling around my feet and legs, I swam back to the steps leading up to the pier. Mom untied me, took her stupid rope and went home—never to reappear on the pier again. This was fine with us.

We could actually dive to the bottom and retrieve freshwater clams, and on occasion, swim with the sunfish, perch and eels.

There were cracks in the pier just below the waterline and we used these as footholds to hoist ourselves up on the pier. On one occasion, I stuck my foot in and disturbed an eel. I shrieked, of course, for attention, and the eel wound itself around my leg a few times and then eventually swam off. After that, I would use the steps to get out of the water.

Almost directly across the road from our house was another farm, a regular working farm with hay, horses, pigs, apples, chickens, dairy cattle and a bull.

This farm had a regular family on it. A mother, father and five sons, who at this time were teenagers. These sons also used the lake to bath in the summer, so it was fun having five teenage boys jumping off the pier and swimming with us whenever they could, usually in the evening when the chores were finished.

On one occasion, possibly a Saturday evening, it seemed there was a dance somewhere and the sons were taking the pickup and going to the dance after the swim, so their best shoes and clothes were toted down to the pier in readiness for the big outing. One of them sassed me about something—he happened to be in the water at the time—and I was on the pier (near his clothes). Without further adieu, I tossed all the shoes and clothes into the lake with him and ''high tailed'' it for home. To my knowledge, it was never mentioned to our mother, nor did I ever learn if the clothes got dried out and pressed in time for the big dance. I did worry about being welcomed into their home for a few days after that, but once I was over my initial fear, I ventured up on the excuse of seeing the newborn piglets and nothing was said about my brattishness.

To have been banned from that farm would have broken my heart. Everything there was so interesting and productive. They didn't have to drink canned milk or eat canned fruit. Mrs. K was the best cook, and the only cook I knew. She sure knew how to fix fresh green beans with real cream and make real berry pies and whipped potatoes with real cream. Their meat may not have been government inspected, but it sure was delicious with gravy and homemade pickles and lots of laughter and chatter at the table. I hardly ever opened my mouth there, except to eat. Mom was never invited but us kids were always treated like part of their family. For Mr. K to smack us on the bottom, call us ''dash nation kids'' and send us home was quite alright with us.

This family rescued us and probably saved our lives many times over. They were so tolerant of us being underfoot, in the oat bin, on the hay wagon, on the tractor, in the hay mow, on the sled with ice for their ice house, in their apple trees and in the pigpen and the manure pile.

Suddenly our house seemed boring. We had no garden or animals, except for a dog and cat. Besides, if we moped around our house, we were put to work at uninteresting chores: keeping that kitchen woodbox full seemed to take up a lot of time; rocking the carriage to lull the baby to sleep; sweeping the wood shed or the barn floor.

Needless to say, Betty and I practically lived outside and up on the Kennedy farm where things were much more interesting.

Things got pretty "interesting" the time I got into their oat
bin, filled with cool oats, and discovered the fun of throwing
the oats out onto the barn floor. Of course, when I got caught,
my reasoning was, there was a rat in there and I was after him.
I doubt I was believed, but Mr. K assured me the rat was gone
and that I could now put the oats back into the bin and then go
home. It was disappointing that I didn't get invited in for a
meal, but I did a good job of cleaning up the oats anyway.

The ice house was the greatest place to play and cool off in
the heat of the summer. During the "dog days" in August, my
mother forbid us to go in the lake because we'd get polio. No
one got polio that I know of, so, since she never seemed to
know where we were anyway, we'd spend our time either in
the ice house or in the lake. The best place to sneak a swim
was to walk around the shore and along to a spot we called the
"Horseshoe."

This Horseshoe had been a gravel pit at one time, but now
was filled with lake water and water lilies. I don't know how
deep it was, but neither Betty nor I could dive to the bottom.

Other than the water lilies, on occasion we'd find freshly
dug spots which were again covered with sandy mud and we
knew we could find turtle eggs if we dug deep enough. The
turtle eggs served as ammunition for any chosen target. We
would find the odd snapping turtle and they were great things
to test. We had to be careful when fooling with them, they
could jump! A long stick was the best tester to see if they were
regular turtles or snapping turtles. Only once were we brave
enough to grab one by the tail and carry it home to show our
mother. She took one look and made us leave it alone. The dog
was curious about it, got too close for a better look and got his
nose nipped. We were glad to see it wander off toward the
lake.

Along the shore behind our house there was a lot of shale rock
which was a great source of fossils. Most of what we found we
could identify as either a leaf or a bug. These fossils were in

excellent condition, but we weren't allowed to keep them at home.

We also discovered a patch of clay. Why Betty claimed this as her own I don't know. I guess owning such a treasure gave her power over me. Bartering with her for clay became a real chore. She was so selfish with it and she was turning out pottery and other magnificent items that I was ready to do or give anything to join in. She hit upon a marvellous idea one day when she discovered the droppings of a rabbit nearby. I had no idea what these little brown balls were, so she had me in her power. A deal was struck! If I would eat five of these balls, she'd share a small portion of her clay. I cooperated willingly: they didn't seem to have much taste anyway.

Well, five small balls of rabbit droppings sure didn't buy much clay! I can only guess how many of these I ate before I had an adequate supply of clay to work with. This control of the clay went on for days, maybe weeks, maybe all summer before she ran out of little brown balls and that was the end of sharing the clay!

By now Betty had started school and I really missed having her around. The baby wasn't much fun to play with and there were no handy neighbours my age, so temporarily, I had to entertain myself. Mom taught me how to knit doll clothes so that occupied my time until Betty arrived home with a fresh supply of school work to teach me. Every evening she was the teacher and I was the pupil. I'm not sure if I enjoyed this activity, but at least I had her undivided attention—plus she liked having the power over me!

Probably by now we had Fred home for a furlough. He would arrive via the mailman. That first visit home seemed like years since he'd left, so he was treated as a guest for the first few days. Mom waited on him, called him "weet" which was short for "sweet." Us kids called him "weet" as well. He dropped his big kit bag in the middle of the kitchen floor and gave chase to Mom (not one of her favourite activities), so us kids would pounce on the kit bag, pull out all his dirty laundry and toss it on the kitchen floor, hoping to find presents. No presents ever appeared, not a one, so we'd go off and leave him and Mom doing whatever they did after a long absence!

Once the novelty of his being home wore off a bit and Mom got tired of waiting on him, she'd start suggesting chores that he could do to help her out. These suggestions would usually cause a fight to break out, which delighted us kids because he'd go outside with us for play.

Play was usually swimming, roaming the beach, catching polliwogs, picking and eating wild berries, identifying wild flowers, birds, trees or visiting a neighbour. Fred taught us wilderness survival as far as what to eat and what not to eat. He also taught us how to tell army time and how to polish his boots and brass uniform buttons. He would have had us pressing his uniform too, if we'd been taller! He put up a swing in the big ash tree we had at the edge of the driveway so that when we got really going good, our feet were right up to the sky. Enough to scare anyone's heart!

Apparently girls were dressed in dresses at all times and I may have had about three dresses altogether. Mainly homemade or ordered through the catalogue. Jumping from the swing when it was at it's highest point was a bit hazardous, since skirts had a tendency to catch on the seat and throw the free fall into a downward spiral. On one such jump, I left the swing at the proper moment only to leave the skirt of my dress still swinging. Once the skirt was disengaged from the seat, it was quietly taken into the woodshed and checked for the proper way to repair the damage. My knitting and doll clothes materials were kept in the woodshed, so needles and thread were readily available for a fast repair job; the adjoining outhouse was the safest place to do this.

Mission accomplished, I walked into the house to see if Mom was going to notice anything unusual about my attire. One look told me I was in trouble! It seems I'd gathered the hem of the skirt onto the bottom half of the top, causing a bit of bulk around the waist. I was forbidden to jump ever again, as the upsidedown dress was removed and repaired in a proper

manner. I was lucky in that I hadn't trimmed any excess
material off with my handy cutting knife.

Doris was now getting old enough to tag along with Betty and
I, which was a bit of a nuisance. With Betty being about six
and Doris barely two, one can understand how she could be
more of a hindrance than a help. Well, if she was going to tag
along, she'd better catch on quick if she was to be accepted
into our world of make-believe and survival.

One of the first things she did to slow us down was fall off
the pier. It was probably one of the very few occasions when
there was someone older with us having a swim. He was a
sixteen-year-old foster child who was staying with the minister
and his wife for the summer.

Doris was in a dress and a pair of underpants and managed
to tumble head first down the pier steps into the water. Betty
and I seemed to know we couldn't help her so as we stood
there watching her bob up and down the young boy, whose
name I believe was David, dove in and pulled her safely out.
Betty took Doris' dress off and laid it on the pier to dry. Once
Doris stopped coughing, she lay down beside her dress and fell
asleep. We continued our swimming until dark, woke her up
and trudged up the driveway promising each other that Mom
must never know. After that fright, Doris did not venture onto
the pier again, but instead stood on the beach and put up a
steady howl while facing us. It seemed to bother us for the first
little while, but the activity didn't really bother us enough for
us to join her on the beach.

One thing she could participate in was the cooking of
crickets and grasshoppers. With stolen wooden matches, some
catalogue pages and kindling wood and a rusted out can, we
prepared the sacrifice. Betty, being six years old, was in charge
of the matches. She put Doris and I in charge of rounding up
the sacrifices and the fire was lit. Once our can of water got
boiling good, we dropped the little critters in one at a time.
This sounds terribly cruel, but we never forgot to pray as each
one was dropped to its doom!

Somewhere around this time, a retired minister started visiting us. I believe he must have just been driving by this first time he came in. The first thing us kids noticed was that he trembled and his voice was shaky. But, Mom was playing hostess and he was invited into the living room to sit in Fred's big rocker right next to Mom's smaller wicker rocker.

Us kids stood in front of him and watched this twitching mass of human flesh and tried not to imitate him and to stifle our giggles. Mom asked us to go play a few times, but we were totally mesmerized and were rooted to the spot. A meal was prepared and he was invited to stay. We were anxious to see this man eat. We were sure our table manners were such that we weren't going to spill our food or drink. Everything was going quite nicely. Mom seemed very proud of us kids being so quiet, but when this poor fellow reached out a trembling hand and said, "Please pass the butter, Molly," it seemed the charade was over! All three of us reached out a trembling hand and in unison said, "Please pass the butter, Molly."

I can't recall if she embarrassed herself by asking us to leave the table, but once the meal was over, he was again invited into the living room and Betty was instructed to get Doris washed up and get her pyjamas on. Betty put warm water into the basin in the sink and instructed Doris to climb onto the chair and onto the ledge of the sink. Doris' coordination wasn't too good that evening and she fell off the ledge onto the chair and down to the floor, screaming all the way. Mom came out, as did our company, to see what the problem was when Betty announced that, "She split where she was cracked." All three of us were told to get our pyjamas on and go to bed.

The first half of the instructions were carried out perfectly, but once upstairs, all three of us laid down with our faces on the register in Mom's room and fell asleep. By this time, Betty and I were big enough to wear army-issue pyjamas. These were issued to Fred in an extra large size, as he was over six feet tall and weighed about 250 pounds. We always took our time rolling up the sleeves and pant legs so that we could sneak around at night and not slip on those slippery floors.

It was this same summer that we experienced our first forest fire. The opposite side of our lake was thick pine forest, and some few miles back from that shoreline, was the coal mining town of Minto. It seems the coal mines caused the fire. The timber was dry, so the fire quickly spread and worked its way down to the shoreline opposite our farmhouse. We could see and smell the smoke at dusk and were hesitant to go to bed that night in case it worked its way around the lake to us. Sometime late that night, Mom got us up to look out our upstairs hall window. Directly across the lake was all ablaze. We watched this for a while, but soon tired of it and left Mom on her knees praying at the window facing the lake and the fire. The rains came that night and the old farmhouse was once again a safe haven, but the opposite shoreline was a smouldering mess of cinders. The coal mines of Minto never did reopen, but the forest, in time, grew thick and green once again.

Once this scare was over, Charlie decided to once again try taking us out in his Model T for some ice cream about three miles down our dirt road to a store. With us three kids, plus his daughter in the back, and he and Mom in the front, we headed down the dusty road.

With cramped conditions, it was necessary we felt, to open the back windows. We tried doing this without their knowledge in the front seat, but each time the car filled up with dust, Charlie would ask us to roll up the windows, which we promptly did, but once he faced forward again, down went the windows.

We were let out of the car to eat this special treat and get our faces washed before getting back in. It was our first taste of ice cream. We were surprised it was so near our house, but without a car ourselves, we couldn't get to it.

One other attempt had been made at having a treat of ice cream, when one winter, Mom decided to make some homemade ice cream. It was a long hard process, what with chipping ice and mixing and grinding on the old ice cream maker that had been left behind in our woodshed. It seems the ice cream was in a container and put outside in the snow to freeze without the lid properly fastened down and our dog discovered it before Mom went to retrieve it. I'm sure that was the dog's first and only feed of ice cream, as the container was licked clean and we were without our special treat. To my knowledge, Mom never tried again. The dog was allowed to live.

All the dogs we ever had were named Trixie. We never numbered them, but that would have made it easier in later years to reminisce about the fate of our dogs.

I believe a batch of fudge met the same fate, only this time it was a different Trixie.

Another game that we allowed Doris to participate in was trying to jump on each other's shadow.

At dusk, shadows become extremely long and slim and the game was to try to jump on each other's shadow before they ducked down. It was like a game of tag, I suppose. These shadows were also very effective when it came to scaring Doris into going home.

Betty would make Doris stand very still and face a treeline that was casting a shadow and point out to her how the shadow was that of any wild beast we could dream up (aliens weren't known of yet) and tell her to watch it carefully, and if it changed shape or moved, she was to tell us immediately. Just the very thought of a beast being in the trees kept her rooted to that spot, plus as the sun set, the shadow would change shape and move forward. By the time Doris came out of her trance and notified us of this, it was time for all of us to head home anyway. She eventually caught on as to what we were up to and she'd go home and tell Mom we were trying to scare her.

We did have some real "beasts." They lived in the lake down behind the schoolhouse. These little beasts were otters and if otters like doing anything, they sure like to play with each other. It appeared they held each other's tails in their

mouths and formed a "line of otters" dipping and diving and
surfacing and frolicking in their play. We could watch this
activity for long periods of time, or until the sun was setting
and we'd head for home before those long shadows appeared
and set Doris off into a howling mood. Years later, someone in
the big city of Fredericton decided our lake had a Loch Ness
monster. It was investigated, but no monster was found.

On one of Fred's visits from wherever he was stationed, he
did buy us some Christmas presents. For Betty and I, there
were two tin trumpets with very rough tin mouthpieces. It was
likely Christmas day or shortly afterwards that Betty and I set
off with our toboggan and trumpets to coast down Chelley's
hill, which really, was only part of the road in front of
Chelley's house. We were moving right along, tooting our
horns with me on the front and her on the back, when we hit a
patch of gravel. Of course, I pitched forward with the trumpet
in my mouth and went face first onto the road. Once I got
screaming really good, I realized something in my crying
sound—like gurgling—and I became aware of blood pouring
down my snowsuit and that there was something in my mouth
that wasn't there before.

After the few minutes walk to my house, I was really
saturated with blood. Poo1r Mom took on a screaming fit of
her own. I was spitting blood on her clean floor when Betty
timidly strolled into the kitchen. She was sent to the
neighbour's to phone for Charlie to come with his car to make
an emergency run to Sussex. Most of what happened next is a
blur, but Mom did manage to get all three of us into Charlie's
car and off we went to the hospital. I believe I was allowed to
sit on Mom's lap in the front seat for the trip. It took seventeen
stitches to put the roof of my mouth back where it had been
scraped clean from the fine bones. Fortunately, these little
bones weren't broken and no teeth were broken. The tongue
was in tact, as well! By the time I was released from the
hospital, the trumpets had disappeared.

A bit about winters in New Brunswick: other than the cold and
wind and snow, one should know there are northern lights that
play and shift like shafts of lights searching the sky at an
airport. The brilliant colours of blue, purple, green, yellow and
orange sway gently and cause the snow to sparkle in faintly
coloured diamonds. A clear cold night of about twenty degrees
below zero is the best time to observe this. While gazing at the
lights, loud booms like gun shots can be heard. This is the ice
contracting on the frozen lakes and rivers. It could also be trees
splitting, as the wood freezes and expands, causing the tree to
split.

The water level under our frozen lake also seemed to
contract and expand and caused huge chunks of quite thick ice
to heave up and form ice caves, particularly along the
shoreline. These were great for a game of hide-and-seek or
even a nap if you were dressed warmly enough. The problem
with the ice caves, was that they formed right at the bottom of
our best tobogganing hill behind our barn. We could get up
great speeds coming down the hill, then hit those ice caves, fly
up into the air, lose our grip on our toboggan and land on these
chunks of ice. Bruised bodies were nothing new. Caves could
also be made simply by digging one by hand in a snow drift.
Also great for tunnels and taking a nap, they were much
warmer than the ice caves.

Usually we had a toboggan and a dog, namely Trixie, that
made the run down the barn hill. Unfortunately, all our Trixies
enjoyed biting our boots when we set out on the toboggan run,
so we always had leaky boots. Sometimes the dog would
miscalculate our speed and accuracy in steering our toboggan
and we'd run over the dog. It was also fun to trek up the hill,
check the imprint in the snow and see if we got a perfect
imprint of a dog being run over by a toboggan!

By now, the ice on the lake would be at least three feet
thick and quite safe for skating. There usually was a pair of
second-hand skates to be found, plus a pair of bob-skates that
we could use.

The ice was clean in patches and very clear. If one laid down on the ice and shielded their eyes, they could see where lamprey eels had attached themselves to the newly formed ice which would be near the surface. Their mouths seemed stretched very open, beautiful pink rimmed with white teeth and the long body hung frozen in a brilliant blue stocking-shape icicle. Why they did this, I never did know. Or even if they survived the winter to swim away when the ice thawed. It was always a mystery to me.

This was when the Kennedy's would harness their work horses with the sleigh and come down to our lake with a chainsaw and cut blocks of ice for their ice house to provide summer refrigeration for their food supply. No reason why us kids couldn't jump on board and enjoy a sleigh ride too. After all, it was our lake and our driveway they were using.

Us kids were usually the first ones on the newly frozen hole to check for reliability the next morning. Thank God it was always well frozen again and could hold our weight.

Another winter activity which never should have been allowed, was the fun of jumping from the pier into the drifts that had formed along the sides of the lake up to the top of the pier. Betty and I would take turns jumping into the drift, going as deep into it as we could, then pulling each other free only to gaze down the newly formed hole to see open water slapping against the lower walls of the pier! God truly looks out for the children.

In the spring, as the ice started to thaw, it would turn a dirty grey colour and get spongy before actually breaking up. Kids must tempt fate and put on the skates and check it out for themselves. This happened one spring day on the brook that ran between Chelley's property and ours. It had to be four feet deep in the creek in springtime and right now, the ice was grey and spongy. I'm getting my skates on to test it, of course, and once on it, it was quite fun. I could bounce on it and hear the rushing water underneath. Betty moved off and onto the nearest bank and watched from a safe distance as I went through the ice up to my armpits, but still not touching bottom. Outstretched arms was all that was keeping me from going down. And Betty, to whom I owe my being alive today, got a log of proper size and length, and laid the log across the ice and encouraged me to climb out. I won't go into detail about how it smarts to have your bare, cold, wet bottom spanked thoroughly for even going onto soft ice. Both of us got soundly spanked ''for our own good.''

Some two or three years later, when the spanking was long forgotten and the lake ice had broken up into huge chunks, just drifting and melting, I tested fate again. This time I was alone!

The water was high and over the pier and ice cakes drifted slowly around in circles on top of the pier. The warehouse door had come off and was drifting with the ice cakes. I got myself a long stick and waded out onto the pier and retrieved the door. I did have on high rubber boots and a heavy wool coat, so I was dressed for a little drifting like an ice cake.

Once on the raft/door, I ''poled'' myself along on top of the pier. Suddenly, my stick didn't feel any pier below me. It was jump and swim or drift off into lands unknown. Jump was the smart decision. A few very hard strokes and I felt the pier below me. I still had my boots on, full of water and the wool coat felt very heavy, but I made my way up the driveway to face the consequences. You would have thought she'd be glad to see me still in tact and alive, shivering and dripping. Not the case at all. I was stripped, spanked again, soaked in a warm bath in the galvanized tub and sent to bed.

Ice flows and rotting ice always made me hesitate after that scare. I often wonder where the door came to rest and if anyone but me knew why it was set adrift.

One other place that was interesting to play in was the upstairs over our combination outhouse/woodshed. Whoever had lived in our house before us had left the upstairs full of packing boxes, muskrat traps, bob-skates, snowshoes, a buffalo robe and what we thought were costumes for Halloween.

These items were stored along the outer walls (in the beginning), mainly because the centre of the floor was not safe to walk on. There were big spaces between the floorboards and the boards themselves were dried-out and loose. To get up there, we needed the ladder leaned against the trapdoor. This manoeuvre was not impossible for Betty and me to accomplish. Once up there, we tested the floor boards. None actually broke—we just had to be careful to not step on an open space between the boards or fall down the open trapdoor.

Since it was forbidden territory, we had to play very quietly and try not to get into a fight over all the treasures. This meant I had to let Betty have first choice of everything. Getting into the clothes was the most fun of all. We imagined these clothes must have belonged to dance hall girls. They were sure different than anything we'd ever seen. We set all the muskrat traps in case someone got up there into ''our things'' that didn't have any right to touch such valuables! We spent lots of time up there.

The safest thing to do, was haul the ladder up behind us and close the trapdoor. That way Mom would have no idea where we were. This secret activity went on all summer, but one day, when Fred was home on furlough, there was some reason why he needed to get up there. First, he noticed the ladder was missing from the woodshed. He was calling out to ''Molly'' as to the whereabouts of the ladder. She came out of the house to show him it was right where it always was—only it wasn't. Betty and I were trapped! Mom found a stepladder and climbed up and tried to push up the trapdoor but it wouldn't budge—not with the weight of two trapped kids standing on it. The jig was up. The ladder was slid down for Fred to climb up, but it seemed things weren't going to be that simple. We knew Fred would just tell us to get down and he'd put things back the way they had been. No such luck! Mom was on her way up first. Betty and I got on opposite sides of the room, so that way maybe one of us could escape down the ladder while Mom pursued the other. Good plan if Fred hadn't been coming up the ladder behind her. It was too far to jump and we already knew the window wouldn't open. A piece of what appeared to be horse harness was taken off the wall and we were threatened with a thrashing when Fred arrived just in time to get a hold of Mom, and us kids were told to get and stay gone till dark. We obeyed promptly. After that, when we pulled the ladder over under the trapdoor, it was only to peer at the neatness of it all and reminisce about the fun with the old clothes.

This was probably the same summer that the Kennedy farm was attacked by crows! There were crows everywhere. And the Kennedy's crops, especially their corn, was being devoured. Scarecrows didn't seem to work anymore. We then discovered the beach was littered with dead crows, obviously poisoned. They must have gone to the lake to drink to try to save themselves from death. Well, there had to be a way to have some fun amid all this death and destruction. Betty and I would give it some thought and come up with some ideas.

The best idea came to us quite by accident. I stepped on one and it cawed, quite loudly. Odd—it was definitely dead. And as we stepped on each crow, it would caw. There was enough dead crows that we allowed Doris to participate. Doris didn't get much satisfaction out of working her section of dead crows because they wouldn't caw like ours. Little did she know we'd already worked on that section the day before, but we told her it was because she wasn't jumping on them hard enough. This extra jumping kept her busy while Betty and I worked on the freshly fallen ones. I believe once the Kennedy's had the farm back under control, they retrieved all the dead (and sometimes well flattened crows—Doris' section) and buried them.

That fall, our father's cousin came to our school to teach. Since she was his cousin, Mom allowed her to get room and board with us. Isabel was all of eighteen years old and fresh out of high school, she may have received what is now called "hazard pay," so she was well qualified to teach all eight grades for a total of about fifteen kids.

Having Isabel live with us made life more pleasant at home. She got a goldfish from somewhere and it swam lazily about its bowl on top of the sewing machine in front of the window that faced the front of the house. It seemed a safe enough perch, but one night us kids got into a baked potato throwing contest (where was Mom?), with Isabel and an odd potato had landed in the goldfish bowl. The poor fish seemed to think it was being fed. Suddenly the thing was floating on its side with its eyes slightly bulging. Betty decided she'd better empty the fish bowl and start fresh, so we wouldn't have to explain why the fish had died and why it's water was so murky. She was doing fine with hot soapy water and in her rush, didn't empty the bowl properly before adding the cold water. The fish didn't seem to appreciate her efforts and continued to swim lopsided. I believe it continued to live and didn't complain about the suds floating on top of it's water.

That summer, Mom had stripped all the old wallpaper off the kitchen walls and repapered with paper ordered from the catalogue. Everything was fresh and clean for the next little while, until one day that fall, when I refused to fill the wood box while Mom was cooking and peeling beets for eating that winter. Well, she was getting a little irate at me, and really, I was just about to give in and do it, when a hot, cooked beet came flying across the kitchen directly at me. Having experience at ducking flying objects automatically, the beet missed me and hit the fresh wallpaper. I moved my butt fast to the woodshed and loaded my arms with wood. Letting myself back into the kitchen with a full armload caused some anxiety, but she was washing that section of wall and ignored me. That section of the kitchen wall always seemed to have a pinkish tinge after that, but I never mentioned it to her.

Betty continued on at school and, by that fall, was in grade two. Her tales of school, her new friend Joy, and getting to walk back and forth with Isabel was beginning to get under my skin, so I started begging Mom and Isabel to let me go to school too. I was promised that on my fifth birthday I could go! I already knew all of grade one work, so there shouldn't be any problem. So, on January 31, I started off to school.

Betty and Isabel were preoccupied with each other. I was ignored, so I trotted along behind, determined to make the best of it. The fact that the odd snowball went flying after them was only what they deserved. It was colder than I thought it should be and it was farther than I thought it should be. Going in the summer to watch the otters was quite different than walking in the cold wind. The road followed the lakeshore, so the wind never let up and my heavy wool snowsuit didn't offer much protection.

My mother must have noticed that I was always half frozen and crying when I came home from school. So with Isabel's help, she decided that since Fred had surplus army issue socks at home, the two of them would make mittens for Betty and me out of them. After all, the long cuffs on the socks would come up to our elbows. The sock was rounded off a few inches below the toe and the extra knitted part was formed into a thumb shape and attached to the hole she'd cut just about where it should be. The completed mitt looked quite nice, what with being sewn together with red yarn. Shortly after the mittens were made, an order came via the mailman with some never-before-seen objects. Here were boys' long underwear with a drop flap in the back and a few pairs of navy blue bloomers. The long underwear went on first, then a combination of elastic straps with garters attached, then the blue bloomers, then the long cotton stockings, a pair of socks, a sweater or two, a skirt or dress, and then the snowsuit. This was a bit better, but not the complete solution. I was still cold.

A problem developed with the blue bloomers! Getting wet from playing in the snow at school caused the blue dye to run into the new long underwear and through to my backside. Well, a blue backside was a small price to pay for the warmth the bloomers provided.

I got to meet Joy. I was not impressed. She and Betty acted
real uppity at school and the other kids were older than me.
Walking home from school with her and Isabel wasn't much
better. I stuck it out and at the end of June, graduated into
grade two—at all of five and a half years old!

By this time, it appeared to me that Mom was getting "fat"
and a bit more irritable.

Betty had been demanding her own room for some time, so
she got to have the room at the very back corner of the house
and Doris came to sleep with me. A bed, secondhand from
somewhere, also came for Betty. It had a fancy metal
headboard, all painted white. There was a couple of spots
where the paint was starting to peel off, and if one looked
really close, it appeared there was a "gold" bed beneath that
paint. We decided a "gold" bed was more elegant than a white
bed, so Betty and I slowly set about removing the white paint,
first in spots where it wouldn't show too much until we
gradually got to the main part of the headboard. Mom at first
thought the paint was just cheap paint and was chipping off by
itself. We went along with the idea that she was right, but
eventually she discovered the neat pile of paint chips and strips
in one corner under the bed. Nothing was done to bring the bed
back to being white or to turn it into the brass bed it had been
at one time. So princess Betty got to sleep in the princess white
and gold bed!

That summer was going to be fun. Isabel would go home to
wherever she came from and I could have some attention. By
this time, Doris and I were pairing up, but she didn't have the
good ideas Betty had for having fun. Swatting at bats with
brooms was one activity in which we could all participate.
Mom wouldn't take an active part in this, but she did allow us
the use of the brooms. We never did hit one, and contrary to
what Mom told us, none ever got into our hair.

Later that summer, when the hawthorn berries were red,
Betty and I set off to pick some to use as ammunition, since
they were not edible. A box was got from the barn and propped

against a fencepost which had a barbed wire attached. I was too short to reach the berries unless I stood on this box. Fred was home on furlough at this particular time, so Mom's attention was taken up with looking after him. Well, as luck would have it, the box flipped and I grabbed for the fence, only to grab onto a barb. I was suspended in space with the barb deeply embedded in the side of my hand and the blood running up my arm and off onto the ground. Betty tried to lift me up to unhook me, but I was screaming to much, so she went to get Fred to help. Getting Fred meant running through the long tall hay behind our barn to reach the house. I'm hung, screaming, and I'm watching the hayfield. Betty, shorter than the hay was tall, wove her way in a zigzag line to the house. It struck me that she could get lost, not being able to see her destination and all. But shortly, out of nowhere, came Fred running toward me. Now I could scream uncontrollably as help was on the way!

A little thing like a three-inch tear in the fleshy side of the hand did not require a trip to the city for repairs. Instead, Mom poured iodine on it (more screaming), pinched the wound together and taped it with adhesive tape. No infection set in and the scar was barely visible by that winter.

One scar that has remained visible came from a trick pulled off by Betty and my being too trusting of her. Mom was sending us to the neighbour's with a small metal shortening bucket for some milk. The ditch beside the road was full of dirty water and mud. It was suggested by Betty that we close our eyes, hold hands and walk blindly along the side of the road. Of course, I closed my eyes tight, just as she did (I'm sure), and the next thing I knew, I'm into the water-filled ditch. Once I climbed out and got my eyes and mouth cleaned out, I am looking to see how she fared through this miscalculation of where the road ends and the ditch begins. She was well on her way, swinging the milk bucket, just as Spic and Span as when she left our house. Well, to keep my punishment to a minimum, I decided screaming was the thing to do, so I headed home looking like the monster from Boogie Creek, I'm sure.

Luck was with me all the way. A convoy of army vehicles was passing through, on its way to Saint John, filled with young army men. The sight of me on the side of the road, head thrown back and howling madly, set off a lot of horn-blowing and hoots as they passed me.

Once at the house, being careful not to get the floor dirty, I remained in the woodshed yelling for Mom. She got down the galvanized tub, got some warm water into it, and with thumb and finger, stripped me down to the bare hide and bathed and changed me. She lay in wait for Betty. I'd told her all of it, plus a little extra, e.g. she pushed me. Betty arrived at dusk, with milk, but no explanation as to her whereabouts. Once cleaned up, it was discovered I'd cut my knuckle on something. More iodine, more screaming. Betty was allowed to live.

This was also the summer we organized a contest and decided to include Doris.

We had a haymow that was empty. Directly below and in front of the side of the haymow, about ten feet down, was the barn floor. The object of the contest was to line ourselves up along the edge of the mow, squat down and see who could pee out onto the barn floor the farthest. The contests would only last a few minutes, as we'd run dry too soon. Doris was good at it, she was double jointed for one thing, so she could thrust her pelvis out further than Betty and I, thus adding an extra inch or two to her stream. We never did get caught at this game, as there was no reason anymore for Mom to come to the barn.

That fall, on November 15th, Mom was ''not feeling well,'' so we were told we were not going to school, but rather we were to walk to the farm next door and stay 'till evening. This was an odd request, since Mom didn't like these people.

The three of us headed out in the direction we were instructed to go. This left Mom home alone and ''sick.'' That worries a kid who really only has one parent at home. Anyway,

that evening, when we arrived back at our own house, we were
shown our new baby brother. I felt I'd been tricked. I sure
would have liked to know how these things happen without my
being aware that such an event was going to take place. Mom
was up and about. The house was warm and water was heating
to bath this new baby. Once she had him in the galvanized tub,
she seemed excited, probably because this baby had something
we didn't have—a penis!

Betty asked a few questions, but didn't seem too
impressed. Her answer to his problem, was that it would
probably ripen and fall off! Simple enough solution.

There was a doctor about twenty-five miles away, who was
always drunk, according to Mom. He was summoned and
arrived about two days later, drunk, according to Mom. She
bundled us up and took us for a walk, leaving this strange
doctor in the kitchen with baby Walter. Much later, when we
returned, the doctor was gone and Walter lay screaming and
wrapped up on the couch in the kitchen. Mom proceeded to
unwrap Walter. His diaper was soaked with blood. This was
pretty scary for us girls. Nothing was explained to us, so we
agreed with Mom, he was a drunken monster.

So that my mother won't be too harshly judged, I will give you
some background on her: she was born in Birmingham,
England, in 1915, about the fifth oldest in what turned out to
be a large family of about ten children. Her name was Amelia
Elizabeth. Before age thirteen, she was either on the streets of
Birmingham, or in their three room walk-up flat with no hot
running water and sharing a toilet with other families in the
same building. Her mother was not well and spent most of her
time in the one bedroom she occasionally shared with what
would have been my grandfather. With their mother being sick
and pregnant most of the time, this left Mom and her siblings
on their own. Mom remembered caring for her baby brother,
George, in the early morning and rushing home from school at
noon, only to find her mother still in bed, so she'd feed the
baby, tend her mother, and help care for the younger children

before heading back to school again. After school, there were errands to run and housework to do.

Her father was seldom home and his fate was never learned, although someone once told the family he had been shot in a "barroom brawl."

The oldest siblings, including Mom, were placed in an orphanage in Birmingham where kindness was not part of the program. But she did have her sister, Doris, there with her and the two comforted each other and dreamed of a better life. Once they were placed in this particular orphanage, they never saw their mother, or other siblings again.

At age thirteen, the two were selected to be sent off "for a better life." Mom to Canada and Doris to Australia. She lost track of Doris at this time, so was totally on her own on a ship with many other "orphans" headed for Canada. The family who chose her, consisted of "two old men" on a farm in a place called Cumberland Bay in New Brunswick. She came with no warm clothing for the climate. She never went to school again, but instead, became a farmhand at age thirteen!

These "old men" were a father and son, ages about sixty and forty. After four years there, the younger man died and the older one told her she was no longer welcome and could "get out."

Word of this spread and she was offered room and board in exchange for "nursing" an old man who was dying at home on another farm a few miles away. She had no choice but to accept. The old man eventually died, leaving a grown son of about age thirty. He was unable to care for himself and at this point, Mom was quite capable of caring for anyone.

She and the son decided to marry and make the best of it. He was to become my father. How they acquired the farm where I was born was either never explained, or I wasn't paying attention at the time. Probably the latter.

Dad's background is vague. He was born at home of a poor farm family with two much older stepsisters, and although he had beautiful penmanship and good spelling I believe he may have had about grade eight education.

One day, when I was about eight, I came home from school to find my mother crying, clutching an airmail letter in her hand. The letter was from a Mrs. Philpott in England and it included a black and white photo of a handsome young man named George.

Mrs. Philpott had adopted George at a young age and she had adored him from the beginning. Mom's tears were of happiness, as she had spent all those years worrying about whatever happened to her baby brother.

Mrs. Philpott and Mom began corresponding and Mom began sending parcels of non-perishables, like sugar, to Mrs. Philpott. To the best of my knowledge, her "baby brother" never did write and it seemed he just didn't want any part of this life or the family he was born into.

Many, many years later, her sister, Doris, in Australia, found Mom too, and that developed into a great long distance relationship. Doris too, was embarrassed about her background, and legally changed her name to Dorothy. Mom was known as "Molly" by now. My younger brother Walter, was named after Mom's father.

But on to more pleasant subjects.

Summers were a series of explorations, endurance tests and just doing our own thing.

One very exciting event happened one windy fall day, when, while walking home from school, it was noticed the air was filled with smoke and cinders. As we walked along, it appeared all this smoke was rising from the general direction of our house. Once we realized this, Betty and I started running home, only to find a tired "bucket brigade" made up of the Kennedy boys and Mom and some passers-by. The hayfield behind our house was still smoking and the back of our cream coloured house was more black than cream. Fortunately, the house was saved. Some time after this Betty and I realized the fire had started on the beach, but the high winds that day had caused it to spread into the hayfield where it got out of control.

These next events are in no particular sequence, but make for a
laugh now: First we will cover the school house, about a mile
up the road from home. This, as we know, was a one-room
building with a woodshed attached at the back and one portion
of the front was a cloakroom or porch. The school was heated
by one pot-bellied stove located in the very centre. We had a
water cooler at the front that was filled daily by one of the
older boys who would carry this water from the farm next
door, sometime before 9 o'clock. The older boys took turns
being responsible for getting to school a bit early in colder
weather to chop the day's supply of wood and get the fire
going before the rest of us arrived.There were about twenty
portable desks arranged up and down beside the stove and
these desks were double, so that two students could share a
desk.

By now, two other little girls about my age were attending
school, so I too, had friends at school and wasn't so dependent
on Betty for companionship. One girl, Evelyn, lived between
our house and the school, but the other lived in the opposite
direction. Evelyn came from a large family. She was third
oldest and had two older brothers. Her oldest brother was
usually the one responsible for the fire in the winter.

One winter day, upon arrival at school, and surely before
the teacher got there, we were witness to a ''contest'' taking
place. The older boys had arranged the desks so that they could
jump from one desk to the top of the hot stove and off onto a
second desk. There was some pretty fancy footwork there for a
while, and they were being encouraged to move the desks back
further from the stove to really test their bravery. Well, the
distance got to the maximum to safely jump, and sure enough,
the stove toppled over, spilling its contents onto all the wet
mittens and boots that had been arranged for drying. The
covers of the stove, too, were on the boots and mittens. Things
were smoking and stinking (nothing worse than the stench of
burning rubber and wool when its wet). Once the boots and
mittens were thoroughly stomped on by all of us, the boys tried

to put the stove back together, which is no easy feat, what with it being hot and time running out.

Things were pretty much back in order when our teacher, Mrs. Gibson, came in. Other than a blackened floor and a lot of smoke, one would never know anything had happened. I'm not sure if anyone was reprimanded for this misfortune or whether she actually ever really knew what caused the stove to collapse.

Mrs. Gibson was elderly. She had grey hair, which was pulled back in a bun, and had grown daughters. One of these daughters eventually married one of the Kennedy boys.

Our school had maps of the world on a pull-down type of blind. Normally, these were in a rolled-up position to expose the blackboards. Of course, all teachers wore dresses in those days and one day, while she was standing close to the unrolled blind giving a geography lesson, the blind suddenly decided to snap up without warning, and also without warning, caught the bottom of her dress and snapped her dress up as well. It caused the dress to tangle into the ''spring.'' Poor Mrs. Gibson, the whole class hooted and no one came to her aid, to there she was at the front of the room with her dress up over her head blindly trying to get the map to release her dress!

I was probably about grade three at this time and was really fitting in.

It was suggested one day at noon (no teacher around) that we girls venture over to the graveyard to check out a fresh grave with flowers and ribbons still in good condition. So we decorated ourselves in flowers and ribbons, most of us had pigtails, and were well under control, when the teacher arrived back from lunch. We thought we were real beautiful, so we innocently marched into the school. Well, our beauty wasn't appreciated and us girls were given an assignment to be completed by the following morning.

I worked very hard on memorizing ''Rhyme of the Ancient Mariner'' that night, but it was too much for me. The next day, none of us could suitably recite the rhyme and we were strapped soundly.

Mrs. Gibson cried. Why, I don't know, but us girls held back the tears as best we could. I wonder if such an impossible task might have been in retaliation for laughing at her with her dress over her head!

Betty was still teaching me at home, and I was picking up a lot of extra information at school as well, because all of us could listen in on all of the lessons being taught. Today I suppose it would be called an "open concept." Anyway, getting back to Mrs. Gibson, she decided the children could plan and organize their own school closing program and the parents would be invited. Not having a clue what to do, I consulted my big sister for ideas. She went through some old books she'd found and decided to teach me to recite from memory in front of the school and parents on closing day. I remember the poem well, because I didn't have a clue what it was about at the time, so I didn't want to screw up:

> *A wonderful bird is the pelican*
> *He can hold in his beak*
> *Enough food for a week*
> *But I don't know how the hell he can!*

Responses were everything from giggles, horror (Mrs. Gibson), gales of laughter, to anger (my mother).

By this time, Betty had developed another hobby, one in which I wasn't allowed to participate. She had got hold of some butterfly books in which she took great interest. She acquired a makeshift net and prowled the field in all her spare moments. Flat boxes lined with cotton batting were used to display her collection. And quite a collection it was.

The specimens were carefully pricked in the head with a pin, dabbed with turpentine, laid out flat on the batting.

They were stashed in her bedroom. I would secretly go in and admire them, but I swear, I never touched them. (Betty specifically asked me to include that swear in this book).

I believe the butterfly books came from Mrs. Philpott in England one Christmas, so her books of specimens didn't really include many that she'd collected. Most of her butterflies were unnamed. Betty said they were too rare to be in any book!

Doris had taken over on the making of doll clothes using my stash of materials.

I decided a project for me would be a snake collection.

Only my snakes were allowed to live. A barrel was provided from the barn and set up in the woodshed. The best place to find and capture snakes was in the wild raspberry bushes near the beach. I can't recall using any protection from bites, so I assume they were non-poisonous.

Some of these treasures must have been up to three feet long. I used a wooden bucket that had a label on it saying "Lard" and my free hand to lure them into the bucket.

Once the dog, Trixie, figured out what I was doing, she was very good at finding snakes and would sniff them out for me and bark at them until I got them safely into the bucket. My collection would accumulate to about twenty snakes, when, somehow, I would find the barrel tipped over and the snakes gone. Remember, our woodshed housed a wood pile in a section that had no floor, so the snakes need only wiggle under the woodpile to be home free. Mom always blamed the dog for upsetting the barrel in the night.

Another event that occurred about this time, was that Mom set to making drapes on her old treadle Singer sewing machine for the bottom of the stairway "to cut down the draught" in the winter.

Material was ordered through the catalogue, of course, and she worked away all fall, as the machine wasn't too dependable. By early winter, she had them neatly hung at the bottom of the steps. They were still fresh and clean that winter and we'd also added a new convenience to our upstairs—a chamber pot (or ''honey pot'' as the neighbours called such things). Anyway, one morning, while Mom bathed Walter, Betty was told to bring down the chamber pot for emptying. Off she trotted and managed to get halfway down the stairs holding the pot with both hands, when she misplaced a foot somehow and fell the rest of the way. The pot came clattering along with her, contents splashed on the papered walls, on Betty, and worst of all, on the new drapes! Mom screamed for me to watch the baby, while she went to see what damage had been done to the new drapes. Betty lay screaming on the floor at the bottom of the steps. Best to fake an injury—punishment was less severe. Walter was rinsed off quickly and dressed and put in the playpen. Everyone's screams had set him off, too. Betty got washed off with the rest of the bath water, the wallpaper got washed with the same water, the steps with the same water and then the honey pot.

Checking drapes for damage, it was decided they could be carefully washed by hand. These drapes weren't really washable, but there was no choice. Once dried on the diaper rack behind the livingroom stove and pressed, they were hung again. Somehow they seemed shorter, so were not going to do the job for which they were intended.

Later that winter, Mom went off with a neighbour who had a car for the day and she took baby Walter with her. We got home from school before Mom got back and we had taken Doris with us that day as this was allowed. Taking a quick look around to see how I could be helpful, I decided that one thing I was good at was cutting. I gave Doris what I thought was a very nice haircut, and with scissors still in hand, thought about how I could make those drapes look better. A fringe all around would make them look rather pretty and besides, the uneven hems wouldn't be so noticeable. This was very painstakingly done, making sure each cut was almost exactly the same distance from the last cut. Up the sides I went, taking the care and precision to do it just right.

Whether or not Mom was angry, I don't recall. Perhaps I blacked out from fear. Anyway, the drapes disappeared for a while only to reappear in the shape of sunsuits for us that summer. And why not—they were already pre-shrunk!

Walter was often put outside in his carriage in the warmer weather for his nap and usually Mom would jiggle the carriage to put him to sleep. She always held on to the handle to do the jiggling, so when I was instructed to jiggle the carriage, I assumed it was to be done exactly as I'd seen her do it. Being short and puggy, I found the handle to be too high, so I made a jump up to grasp the handle and get on with the responsible job of putting the baby to sleep. Somehow, the carriage came over on top of me and the baby lay sprawled and howling on the ground.

If I hadn't been pinned beneath the carriage, I'd have made a run for a safer place, but no such luck. I was stuck. Walter was checked for damage before I was released and a spanking was administered before she took over the jiggling.

Walter was a bit of a nuisance, just as Doris had been! Another thing he had that we didn't, besides a penis, was a beautiful head of blond curls. You can guess what happened to those curls one day when her back was turned! Retaliation, maybe?

That winter, we had tons of snow again and our cat had a batch of kittens, maybe three or four, which were housed in a box with some old towels in the woodshed.

Our cat, and we only ever had the one, was inappropriately named Scotty. She went off one day, before the snow really hit, to Kennedy's barn to search for mice, no doubt, leaving her still nursing kittens behind. By late afternoon, she hadn't returned and we checked the kittens and begged Mom to let us bring in the box and all to put behind the kitchen stove for warmth. She allowed us to do this and Betty prepared her doll bottle with some warm milk and fed them. They were fine when we went to bed, but still no Scotty and we were worried she'd been lost trying to get home in the storm. As luck would have it, the kitchen fire went out during the night and the kitchen got terribly cold. In the morning, the little kittens were blue and stiff. Betty gently gathered them up, detected a faint heartbeat and passed the kittens around for gentle massaging while Mom got the stove going again. A miracle was taking place, the kittens began to meow and squirm and a doll bottle was prepared again.

They nursed and were fine by noon. Scotty meowed at the door by mid-afternoon and she too was welcomed in and allowed to carry on her motherly duties. Thus, those kittens had used up one life before they were a week old.

Kittens were usually given away to neighbours to be barn cats. Cats lived on mice and birds in those days. Scotty remained with us and kept the field mice to a minimum.

With Betty and I being pretty well independent of each other now, we were allowed to walk to the other neighbours' to play with their children.

Evelyn's house was fun for me. Her Mom was a heavy set lady with curly red hair, who was always singing and laughing. There was always a nursing baby in that house and her Mom never hesitated to produce a well-freckled boob to nurse the little tykes. One thing you had to be careful of in that house, was always to check where you were about to sit down. She kept her babies in the kitchen wrapped in blankets on the kitchen cot.

There was always bread—either baking, cooling or rising—and plenty of molasses to dip freshly-baked bread in for a snack.

Evelyn's Dad was a carpenter and farmer, and he had a team of workhorses and fields of vegetables. They didn't have much money or anything else, but they were a happy crowd.

We had to pass their house on the way to school. One morning as we passed, a bedroom window was thrown up and out came a cat. It landed on all fours and walked away from its unexpected flight from the second storey window. When Evelyn caught up with us, we asked what that was all about and she explained that her father had put his foot into his slipper only to discover the cat had done its bathroom ablutions there first and it upset her Dad. This was good for a laugh all the way to school.

Between Evelyn's house and ours, was another farm and they didn't like us. And it seems Mom didn't like them. Us kids had no opinion whatsoever, but being loyal kids, we didn't spend a lot of time there, although it was the farm we spent the day at when our brother was born.

This farmer had two teams of horses for ploughing and whatever else you use horses for when you don't have a tractor. Maybe that's why Mom didn't like them—they didn't own a tractor! Anyway, one evening when his horses were finished their work and neatly tethered in their stalls for the night (did you know horses sleep while standing up?), I ventured over. Sure enough, the barn doors were closed and all was quiet. Easy enough to lift the latch and go into the barn to see exactly what horses do during the evening when they're not working. All four turned to look at me—gee, they're big! I wandered up to horse number one. He let me look him over. I could see the rope of his tether was loosely tied. He let me untie him and he just stood there. Horse number two was just as unconcerned as horse number one. I untied him and he just looked at me. Horse number three, same thing. And horse number four. All just standing there looking at me. It wasn't as interesting as I thought it would be, so I just walked out and latched the door behind me. No need to explain my whereabouts—no one asked and I didn't volunteer.

You know the criminal is supposed to return to the scene of the crime? Well, return I did, the next morning. The barn door was open and the farmer was in there doing something with a big needle shaped like a hook with some heavy duty thread attached. One horse in stall number one had some odd looking stitching on his rump; horse number two seemed to have some wounds as did the other two. They were all tethered neatly again patiently waiting to be stitched up.

The farmer was not in a good mood that day and just glared at me. I slowly backed up until I was once again out the door and bolted for home, only I didn't go in the house—I went into our quiet barn where everything was neat and orderly and there was no living thing in there except me.

How long I thought I could stay there before being missed was about to be tested! A real long time passed, I got hungry and chewed on some dried hay strands and still no one came looking for me. I wondered off to the beach, no one there. I walked around to the Horseshoe, no one there. I was bursting to confess! Finally, Betty came looking for me. I wasn't talking too much, dragging me feet as I walked along behind her to the house. Boy, was I hungry! No one had contacted Mom about the disaster next door.

It was like the expression "waiting for the other shoe to drop." It never dropped, but I worried a lot. Since this farmer had put me under so much stress, I felt the need to retaliate. His corn stocks were high and they came right up to our property line in neat rows, a long way from his house and barn. I think I hit on an idea! Why not straddle each row of corn and mow them down? Well, maybe not mow, but at least break them a bit. It was hard work, but I managed to get through quite a few rows before I tired of the game and wandered off again. So now farmer D: you know for sure who untied your horses that night and, if you noticed your corn stalks broken, who also did that deed! I feel better now for having confessed.

By now Betty's friend Joy, from school, was old enough to ride her bike the whole three miles to our house. She usually brought her bathing suit and she and Betty would get really uppity and leave me out of their activities. They hid themselves in our haymow and talked of private things or just plain sneaked around trying to avoid me.

We still had our chicken house behind the main house and it had been cleaned and disinfected. We periodically used it to play in and stash any contraband that wasn't safe in the house. The chicken house had a latch on the outside of the door and one window that wouldn't open. Betty and Joy concocted some story about playing with me in the chicken house and lured me in. They shut the door behind me and latched it. They were on the outside and I was on the inside with no way to get to the outside! They just laughed at my screams and they went off to the pier for the afternoon. When they finished their swim and Joy was on her bike again heading home, Betty unlatched the door and let me out. What a fool I was. By now I should have known my older sister was not a nice person.

Amelia "Molly" Young. 1933

The family farm at Young's Cove, Grand Lake, N.B. 1940

Jean, Betty, Joy, Diane and Doris. 1943

Jean, Betty and Doris Young. 1944

Jean and Walter Young. 1943

Goldie Smith. 1944

Betty, Goldie, Doris, Jean and Walter. 1943/44

Young's Cove Road School. Front: Diane Bamford, Jean Young, Evelyn Moss, Donnie Moss, George Chapman. Centre: Paul Gale, Shirley Cox, Harold Dykeman, Ashley Duffy, Stanley Moss, Joy Bamford. Back: Harold Moss, Lorna Chapman, Hazel Chelley, Frank Barton and Betty Young. 1945

Jean Redekopp

The Youngs: Jean, Amelia "Molly", Betty, Walter and Doris. 1945

Snow removal and the Kennedy farm. 1943

On McNabs Island, Halifax Harbour

Fred was tranfered to Halifax: only not right in Halifax, but rather on McNabs Island in Halifax Harbour. He was no longer in the Service Corps, but in the Provost Corps.

McNabs Island had forts and an army barracks so he was stationed there to guard Canadian army prisoners that had broken whatever rules applied when you're a Canadian soldier.

It was decided that the whole family would move to McNabs Island and that fall—I believe about 1945/46. Fred had taken Trixie, the dog, for company at the barracks ahead of the rest of the family.

Suddenly, we were on a train heading for Halifax. Yes, the train really did exist.

It was awfully long and confining, and it must have been late at night when the train pulled into the Halifax station. It seemed there was no roof on this place (of course not, it was the platform for loading and unloading passengers) and Fred was not there.

Us kids had been sleeping on the train. Mom woke us to disembark which, of course, set us all off howling. I could sense panic in her voice as the train blew it's whistle and pulled out again. Suddenly, Fred appeared and we were into a taxi headed for a hotel for the night. Fred stayed with us that night, but he had to catch the little army boat over to McNabs

Island early in the morning which left us on our own in this big city.

Gee, the hotel room had taps and running water and electricity and carpets and an unused fireplace and a bathroom with the biggest bathtub I'd ever seen. In fact, the only real bathtub I'd ever seen.

Mom went to the dining room and brought back some juice and muffins. We ate in our room. We all went out that morning to explore our surroundings. It was sure different from home. All these cars and oxen and cobblestone streets and streetcars that ran on tracks and so many people. I hadn't realized that there were that many people in the whole world. I presume Mom shopped, while us kids just gapped at our surroundings.

We returned to our hotel sometime during the day, ate again and then she, for whatever reason, decided to go out again. Us kids were to remain in the hotel room and be quiet.

I'm sure Betty was in charge—after all she would have been about nine years old! Once Mom was gone, we decided to see just how much water was in those taps and a water fight ensued. We found some tomatoes in Mom's stash of groceries and then a tomato fight ensued. Doris had been a sitting target perched on the bed that was directly in front of that fireplace. Whether we got a direct hit or whether she tried to escape behind the bed is unclear, but suddenly, she was down behind the bed pinned between the fireplace and the bed, screaming her head off. We were trying to pull her up when a knock came on our door. Dead silence from within for a moment. Then we heard a voice say "quiet down in there."

Once we got Doris out of her trap and onto the bed again, we discovered the fireplace had been used. There was soot all over Doris and now it was on the bed. There were tomato spatters on the wall and tomato pits were lazily sliding down the wall.

Very early, possibly before daylight the next morning, we left our hotel room and headed for the little army boat. The trip took about 20 minutes and it was my very first boat ride (I'm

not counting my adventure on the warehouse door amid the ice
chunks). We landed at the dock apparently at low tide, since
the only way onto the dock was to climb up a long ladder.
Mom wasn't used to such hardships as climbing a ladder in her
only pair of high heel shoes. Fred should have arranged for a
high tide. So off we went, up to the narrow gravel road that ran
directly across in front of the army barracks and trekked our
way along, on foot, about a half mile to our ''cottage' where
we were to stay for the winter.

    We were now anxious to see Trixie, but were told by Fred
the sad news that she jumped off the dock the day before and
tried to swim after Fred while he was on the little boat. She
must have drowned, because she was ''lost at sea.'' It would
be our first time without a dog and we were very sad.

Our cottage was similar to the farmhouse, but not nearly as
big. There was no running water, no electricity and no
bathroom. It was adequately furnished and a handpump was
outside beside the back door. The outhouse was down over the
hill behind the cottage in the woods! Well, well, this was
home. We got to choose our own beds upstairs while Mom and
Fred claimed the bedroom on the main floor.

    There were no cars on the island, except for a jeep that
went between the two lighthouses. It belonged to the
lighthouse keeper that tended both lighthouses on opposite
ends of the island.

There was a one-room schoolhouse that housed all eight
grades. Our teacher was allowed to use the little army boat as
her transportation from the mainland. There were a few other
cottages on the island, but we were the only army family,
therefore, the only family allowed to use the boat. There was
no store.

    The next day, we were sent off for our first day at our new
school and to meet a whole bunch of new kids—ten to be
exact. Close to nine o'clock, our teacher came trudging along
looking very much like Mrs. Gibson! She seemed surprised to

see us, the new kids that she hadn't known she was going to have, and acted like ten was the maximum she was prepared to teach. Doris was in grade one. It was her first experience at school, so she'd brought along her cut-outs!

I guess the day went reasonably well. We walked home for lunch, but no one walked with us. Going back after lunch, we discovered a shortcut through the woods and chose that route, so the other kids wouldn't stare at us. I guess we were a bit of a novelty, being an army family and allowed to use the boat sort of put us in a class above them. There were maybe eight families on the island. A couple of families had boats of their own and the other families depended on them for their trips to the mainland.

School itself was uneventful, except for one thing. There were times when the weather was stormy and the ocean was choppy and our little boat either didn't make the trip, or would be running late. We could watch the passage from a clearing near the school to see if the boat was coming. If the boat was even five minutes late, us kids would all take off, tell our parents the teacher didn't arrive and we'd have a holiday. Since there were no phones on the island, the poor teacher would arrive late, only to find no kids in sight and no way to round us up, unless she was to go door knocking and she wasn't about to do that.

These free school days were used to explore the forts, abandoned since the war was over and the Halifax mainland no longer required their protection from an invasion. An invasion of what, I'm not quite sure.

On one of these free days, it was decided that Betty could take me over to the mainland to see a movie. How exciting. My very first movie.

We boarded the boat, got off again on the mainland and went this way and that way to a theatre. We saw Bing Crosby in *The Bells of St. Mary's*. I was so enthralled with it all. It was surely the greatest thing ever invented. Back onto the boat and home, safely in the care of a nine-year-old.

McNabs Island was also home to about forty ponies that roamed freely during the winter months. During the summer, they were part of the Bill Lynch Show---a travelling carnival.

These beasts were testy. I don't believe I ever got brave enough to approach one of them. They did give me a scare one night after dark when I had to use the outhouse down over the hill. I set out alone with the flashlight, down the path in the woods and got inside the outhouse. While I was in there, the ponies suddenly appeared outside, rubbing on our outhouse and causing it to vibrate and jiggle. They were using our outhouse to scratch themselves. I was afraid that the outhouse and I would topple over and roll the rest of the way down the hill to parts unknown. For a long while, I yelled for Fred (I knew Mom wouldn't come down there after dark), but no one in the house heard me.

Finally, Fred came looking for me. I was a mound of weeping, wailing flesh when he pushed open the door to peer into the dark and retrieve me.

McNabs Island also had some unique animals[x] other than squirrels. There was one what looked like a crossbreed of cats and rabbits. These things were about the size of a rabbit, but did not have long ears, but ears more like that of a cat with about the same sized head as a cat. Their fur was more like a rabbit and they had the long back legs of a rabbit and they did a short hop. They were wild and nibbled their food like a rabbit. Fred had a name for these, but I've long since forgotten it. And indeed they were not a cross of cat and rabbit. I have never seen these anywhere else, nor have I ever heard anyone say they'd seen such an animal. Their little tails were also similar to a rabbit. Try as we might to catch one, we never could.

The island also had snakes. They were easy to catch!

There was lots of snow that year too, and the wind off the ocean blew. Our trail to school was through the woods, so we had some protection from it. As I mentioned before, the ocean

x MANXES

got pretty rough for the little boat and one day, while making the crossing, it was exceptionally rough. The water was spraying onto the boat and the breakers were rolling into the back of the boat. It was like a small fishing boat with an unprotected back half. The wind and waves were rocking it wildly and the water was spraying the windows at the bow where we were. Mom started to panic halfway across and dropped to her knees and started praying. I'm sure if she hadn't been there that us kids would have preferred to be in the stern of the boat enjoying ourselves in the spray. We made it safely, but when it came time to return to the island, Mom was a bit apprehensive to say the least. We were such brave kids, you'd have thought she'd have trusted our judgement more.

By now, we were getting to know the other kids on the island. I wouldn't swear to it, but I believe all the families were squatters. None of the cottages had basements and it seemed very few of the fathers (except mine) went to work. One family nearby befriended us. They had a girl named Gloria who was my age and a boy named Bernie who was about two years younger. They were shy kids and their family consisted of the mother, the grandmother, Gloria, Bernie and a younger brother. They did have a father who "worked on the boats" and was seldom home. When he did come home, he wrecked havoc because he'd get drunk and beat up the family.

On one such occasion, he managed to upset the woodstove and set their cottage on fire. Fortunately no one lost their life and they continued to live there with that end of the house boarded up. I never did see Gloria's father in all the time we lived there.

There was another family on the opposite end of the island whose name was McNab. They had two little kids—very shy and sweet. Since they had the same name as the island, we treated them with respect!

Then there were the Perrons, Hurleys, Deveaus, Carrons, Lynch and Holland and a family that only stayed about a month named Roach.

The Holland's and us got off to a very bad start. The oldest boy was probably a teenager and was very tall. He didn't go to school. Next there was Vergie and somewhere in the middle was Violet and more younger kids who simply played in the mud and snow all the time.

The oldest, Billy, somehow managed to pin me against a shed between the two properties and pelted me with crabapples about the first week we were there. Well, since he was too big for me to tackle, the next best solution to this problem was to attack Vergie. She was about right in size for fair combat. I got my chance one day walking home from school when, for no good reason, she hit me over the head with her books, and her books and pages went flying. This happened fairly near our house and there was a fence right there, so I ducked under the fence, grabbed some of the books and pages and started running for a safer place, namely home. Vergie started to crawl under the fence to give chase. She got caught on the fence, belly down on the ground. I came to a halt when I realized she couldn't free herself. I slowly and with great caution, approached the yelling kid, and once I checked out her predicament and knew she'd be there for a while, I raised her books above my head and gave her a sound thrashing on her head. Then I threw the books at her and walked off.

Mrs. Holland came over and yelled at all of us, but Mom stood her ground and yelled just as loudly. We didn't interfere with them after that.

According to everyone that had lived on the island for a while, it was haunted and it did have a few strange phenomenon. We had been told about the "burning ship" that would pass between the island and the mainland. Sure enough, one day Mrs. Carron came running over to our house because the ship was passing through at that moment. We all gathered out behind our house, and sure enough there was a ball of fire on the water in the shape of a burning ship. We watched it for quite some time as the sun went down. Once the sun dropped behind the trees, the ship faded to nothing. Very exciting stuff.

We had a boarder named Bob, who had a dog, and this man was responsible for making a couple of trips down to the army barracks during the night to put coal in the furnace. On one such occasion, he and his dog headed out in the middle of the night to do his job and sometime during the night, the dog returned alone and whined to be let in. Much later, when it had already started to get light outside, Bob came in, obviously shaken. He sat down at the table and started to explain: while walking along the beach with the dog, an apparition suddenly appeared—a crying woman sitting on a rock. Bob and the dog had started to approach her when the dog yelped and ran off toward our place. Bob continued to approach her. He could hear the whining, when suddenly, she just evaporated. This episode upset him a lot and we noticed the dog wouldn't go out again after dark. Soon after this, Bob took up drinking. Mom was against that, so when Bob challenged my three-year-old brother to a boxing match, Bob was given his notice to vacate our premises.

One reasonably warm day, Mom decided to go to the mainland and therefore, sent Walter off to school with us girls. The school also seemed to serve as a babysitting service. For some reason, I didn't go back to school that afternoon, pretended to be sick, and crawled into the big bed in Mom's bedroom on the main floor and caught a nap until Betty, Doris and Walter came home. They got home before Mom, so we were alone.

The coal fire in the kitchen stove had burned almost out and Betty tried to get it going to warm the place and have it ready for Mom to cook supper. Since it didn't catch right away, she decided to pour in some coal oil and again put the lid on. There must have been some hot coals in there because, suddenly, KABOOM!—the covers of the stove flew up and hit the ceiling, the house shook, there was soot all over the kitchen and it didn't smell so good in Mom's bedroom either.

For some reason, Bernie showed up, but because we couldn't have anyone in if Mom wasn't home, we refused to let him in. He sensed we had a ''secret'' and demanded to be let in. No way. By now we were trying to clean up the soot.

He found a plank somewhere nearby and heaved it through the window of Mom's bedroom and it landed on Mom's bed where I had been just moments before! So now we had a broken window, a plank on Mom's bed and dirty snow and mud in her bedroom as well as a kitchen full of soot! Thank God, Fred got home first and was ready to protect us. As a reward for his bravery in facing up to Mom, we thought we'd learn to call him Dad, since he was now living with us and he was our Dad—he'd just proven that.

The following photos taken on McNabs Island are now deposited in the Public Archives of Nova Scotia in Halifax.

Jean Young, Peter and Nancy McNab, with Fort McNab on hill at right.

Betty, Jean, Doris and Walter inside the fort at St. Ives Point.

Doris and Walter on large cannon inside the fort at St. Ives Point.

Group photo from McNabs Island School on Old Military Road. The students include: Donnie Hurley, Francis Deveau, Gloria and Bernie Betts, Virginia and Voilet Holland, Eileen Hurshman, Margaret Roach, Nancy McNab, Reggie Cleveland, Doris Young, Jean Young, Betty Young and Walter Young.

Walter sitting on a pony from the Bill Lynch Show with Bill Lynch or one of his brothers holding the pony's head.

Back to the Farm

The winter passed by only too quickly and we were soon ready
to head back to the farm in New Brunswick. Dad would be
driving us home with a 1943 Chrysler he'd bought. On the way
home, we came across a moose on the side of the road and
Mom demanded he stop the car for a picture. Mom was behind
the car, apparently in his blind spot, with the camera at ready.
But before she could snap the picture, Dad backed into her and
sent her sprawling on the side of the road. The moose took one
look and wandered off. Us kids were so disappointed she
didn't get her picture of the moose! For the rest of the drive
home, there seemed to be a one-sided conversation in the front
seat with Mom doing all the talking, quite loudly!

Back at the farm, the front windows were boarded up and
the door was unlocked. All our possessions were still there just
as we had left them. It was springtime again and the grass was
getting green, the peonies out front were starting through the
earth and we were a happy bunch. We sniffed the air. No salty
smells here, just wet fresh earth and fresh grass. We settled in
again, got another Trixie, and Scotty came home from
Kennedy's barn glad to see us. This was likely 1946.

Dad stayed for a few days and left again on the train for
Halifax, leaving the car behind for Mom to learn to drive.
Charlie was selected to teach her, so one evening about dusk,
along came Charlie with his daughter (there was no mother in
the family—she had passed away shortly after giving birth to

Goldie). Mom got behind the wheel and Charlie got in the passenger's seat. Us four kids, plus Goldie, got in the back seat. Now, you must understand that Charlie talked very slowly and Goldie hardly talked at all, even when we gave her the chance. So here we go. Charlie is instructing Mom about shifting and the clutch and explaining the whereabouts of the brake. Of course, it's dark in the car, so Mom is driving slowly and listening, but not able to see where these things are located. Suddenly Charlie started to speak, ''There's a car parked...'' when Mom jerked the car hard to her left and missed the parked car on the side of the road, but managed to drive the car into a driveway and right into a woodpile where it stalled.

Charlie was just finishing his sentence as we stalled out. No one came out of the house to see who ran into the woodpile, so Charlie instructed Mom how to restart the car, put it in reverse and get back on the road. The rest of the evening was uneventful, but I believe the rest of the driving lessons were done during daylight, with just Charlie and Mom in the car.

Other than going for the odd ice cream down the road, the car didn't go too far at first, but she got braver as the summer wore on. She had a tendency to panic, hit the brake hard, send us kids slamming into the back of the front seat, and throw her hands up in horror.

One day, we set out with Mom, Evelyn's mother with nursing baby, and us kids in the back seat. I can't recall where we were going, but I do remember we had to stop for gas. Mom warned Evelyn's mother ahead of time in case she wanted to tuck the freckled boob back into her dress or detach the baby from it at least. This was ignored and as a young man came to tend our needs, he stared at this lady with the nursing baby as he pumped our gas. Maybe that's why I don't remember where we were going, because I was too interested in what was happening in the front seat!

Our car developed a wobble, so Mom would drive slowly instead of taking it to a service station. We headed out for Sussex one day in the wobbly car and got there safely enough, but on the way home, as we pulled away from an intersection, the front side of the car on the driver's side dropped down and there was a scraping sound. Would you believe it, there was our front wheel rolling along beside us! Someone stopped and retrieved the wheel and somehow we were on our way again with the wobble cleared up! I think the car sat in the driveway for a long time after that.

Mom never did have a driver's license—she didn't know she needed one. When Dad came home later that summer, the car wouldn't start. He flagged someone down in a gravel truck and asked to be towed. Well, I wanted to get in the car with him to steer and he said "no." Being determined, I waited and watched as the towrope was attached to our front bumper and Dad was inside and had given the truck driver the signal to go ahead. That's when I got on the running board of our car on the passenger side and squatted down with a fairly good grip on the door handle. Dad couldn't see me, so off we went. The dust was very thick and it seemed we were really speeding along and I was losing my grip and getting very scared. Without further adieu, I straightened up and peered into the window at him. He sure looked surprised and started blowing the horn like crazy, but the truck driver didn't seem to hear. By now I knew I had to save myself, so with one great heave, I pushed myself away from the door and went flying over and over, only to come to rest in the ditch. I was unhurt, but dirty. The truck and our car sped away with the dust rolling out from underneath. I walked home, a relatively short distance. I remember wishing it was longer, so Dad would come back and protect me. No such luck. On top of that, Mom had seen me attached to the door handle from out of our kitchen window, but lost sight of me once the dust got really rolling.

By now our road was being widened and it seemed it was going to become part of the Trans Canada Highway. Gravel trucks came and went and the dust rolled like crazy all summer.

Part of our frontyard was taken away and the road was closer to our house. We often heard the sound of dynamite blasts. Mom waited until evening to hang out the washing and would retrieve it in the wee hours of the morning before the trucks started again.

Betty and I made friends with some of the young fellows driving the trucks and they'd often stop in front of our house and blow the horn for some company in the cab. It seemed Betty's friend always told her what time he'd be by and she would put on some of Mom's earrings and some lipstick and wait for her ''date.''

These guys would share their lunch with us, treat us to pop and keep us with them pretty well for the day. How exciting for us at ages ten and eight to have such a good time.

We ran into a snag, though, and it was their fault.

It seemed Mr. Chelley had asked the guys to drop off their empty dynamite boxes at his barn to be used as cattle feeder boxes. We didn't know Mr. Chelley had asked for them and we saw them piling up beside his barn. We took an armload home with us one day and just set them adrift to see which way they'd drift. Once they were missed, Mr. Chelley came storming and raging to our house and lit into Mom about it and she had no idea what he was talking about. He threatened to call the police (what police?) if we ever set foot on his property again. We told our friends, the truck drivers, about it and they had a great laugh.

Mom got to know the names of our regular guys and she'd give them a bit of home baking and refill their Thermos with good, cold water.

It was a great summer. Plus we'd been picking strawberries that summer at Kennedy's and earned some money, not to mention getting to eat our noonday meal with them and their cousins who had come to help with the crop.

Their strawberry patch was far enough back from the road that it didn't get full of dust, so we could eat our fair share as well without getting a mouthful of dust. We did such a great job with the strawberries that we were promised more work when the potatoes were ready to be dug that fall.

The cousins were mainly teenage boys as well, and one, about sixteen years old, could play the guitar and sing. Betty sure had a crush on him. She'd croon along like a sick cow. Then there was Leonard, about twelve years old. He was getting paid a dime every time he could catch me and kiss me. I hated that stuff! I preferred to get nailed in the rear end with a fat, juicy strawberry and just have a good old strawberry fight. And there was a girl, the exact same age as me, same day, same year!

Later in the summer, just as promised, we were part of the potato picking crew. The digger, pulled by the tractor, would dig up the potatoes with the tops still attached and it was our job to go behind the digger and shake the potatoes loose and toss the stocks into the path separating the rows. Someone else would take the stocks away. This was back-breaking work, but we knew Mr. Kennedy was depending on us and he was paying us. Leonard was again earning those extra dimes!

The odd potato fight would break out and they hurt worse than the strawberries. Once the potatoes were all in at the barn in a great pile, it was time to start bagging them. My job was to count the bags as they were tossed on the back of the truck for market. Every once in a while, Mr. Kennedy would say, ''I make that 22 (or 35). How many did you count?'' and my total was always exactly the same as his! He was amazed that I always had the same total as him!

That fall, I had $32! I decided to buy a skating dress I'd seen in the catalogue, for one thing. One day before school started, Mom decided to take us to Sussex in our car so we could spend our money and get some school clothes. We, Betty and I, were dropped off at the movie theatre and Mom and our siblings went off to shop. After the show got over and we wandered outside to meet Mom, I discovered all my money was missing! I was so sure I had it rolled up in my hand during the movie and now it was gone! My whole future down the tubes! Guess what I set about doing? Yes, howling! Right there on the streets of Sussex. Mom explained to the man at the theatre and asked if we could please go back in to look for the money. He let us do this, but the theatre was darkened now and we had no idea where we had sat, so the money was gone for good. Mom bought me a blue sweater with white stars that day. I picked it out. And, not too long after that trip, a parcel came through the mail for me. In it was the beautiful red skating dress.

I mentioned before that Kennedy's farm had dairy cattle as well as a bull. Betty, during the summer, had asked her truckdriver friend what good the bull was since it didn't give any milk. He had thought it a terribly funny question, so she was too embarrassed to pursue it further.

Betty and I were walking along our dusty road one day on our way home from school and there was the bull in the pasture beside the road. Its horns had either been cut off or shed. Anyway, there was blood and the bull was in a bad mood. Having nothing better to do, we stopped and watched him pawing the ground and snorting and looking right at us. We decided to throw some stones at him to make him go away. We had pretty good aim. We hit him a couple of times, and instead of going away, he just got more upset. Suddenly, he started coming right in our direction. We didn't wait to see if he'd stop at the fence. There was a really deep ditch here and, in my haste to get safely out of the way, I missed my footing when I tried to jump across and I landed on my back in the ditch. A view of the bull's belly was directly overhead for a moment. I stayed there very quietly in case he came back. All was very quiet, so I stuck my head up to see where Betty had got to. I couldn't see her, but I did see the bull near the beach. He had his head down and was snorting. I was sure he had Betty on the ground killing her. Oh, Lord, how was I ever going to explain this to Mom.

Suddenly, a voice from up top of the only birch tree, in fact the only tree in sight, called down asking where the bull had got to. Once I assured her all was safe, she came down as far as the bottom limb and then got scared to come the rest of the way. She was going to have to jump down and it had to be a

good ten feet to the ground. To this day, Betty can't explain
how she ever got up that tree! The bull was somehow put back
into Kennedy's barn. It was there—I checked the next day.

One night that fall, Betty developed a terrible pain in her
abdomen and lay on the cot in the kitchen with the hot water
bottle on her stomach and groaned. The next morning she was
terribly sick, but the actual pain seemed to have subsided.
Mom diagnosed it as appendicitis. It was arranged for Betty to
go into the hospital, probably in Sussex, and have it removed.
    Did we did take her in our car? I don't recall. Anyway,
once Betty was fixed up and home again, Mom decided it was
my turn, so I was carted off to the hospital and had mine
removed. Then it was Doris' turn, and once she was all fixed
up, Mom started at the beginning again and had all of us
readmitted to have our tonsils out. After all, we had a steady
income and what better way to dispose of it than to have your
kids properly fixed up?
    During our recuperation, we discovered that Mom's white,
sparkly figurines tasted like salt and alum. As a comfort food,
we'd suck on these figurines (behind her back, of course) until
all the figurines were mere blobs of faceless ladies. She
discovered the disfigurations one day and said to herself out
loud—how they were evaporating. We all agreed. They were
indeed evaporating.

A lot of other foreign foods were getting into me as well. I was
the only one who had to be treated every summer with
powdered, purple pinworm medicine. That had to be the most
horrible tasting and hard to swallow stuff in the world. Why
Mom didn't make a paste out of it is beyond me. My protests
didn't allow me to think of doing it either—escape was
uppermost on my mind. It was purple and it stained my lips
and mouth and the front of my clothes.
    (Years later when I saw the movie *One Flew Over the
Cookoo's Nest*, Nurse Ratchet with her medication for those
poor patients reminded me of Mom trying to get that medicine

in me). This treatment only took place in summer and fall. Of course, I never admitted to eating clover heads, rose petals, grass, hay and oats and those little ''pineapples'' that grew on creepers everywhere. We never washed any wild berries we'd find in our travels either.

One summer day, in our quest for berries, we noticed a big beautiful bird taking something in it's mouth to the old hollow stump down on the beach. She was so big and coloured yellow, tan, white and brown. We watched her for days and days and suddenly there seemed to be young ones in there, too. They started poking their little heads out for her. We never went too close, though, until one day, when Joy was visiting and she stuck her arm into the hole and retrieved a beautiful ''flicker'' woodpecker. She gently handed it to Betty, and went back for a second one. I didn't get to have one. Wasn't that just like Joy to leave me out! They took their new ''pets'' home. Mom had never seen such a bird and helped Betty with it. We had it in the kitchen in a box (it still couldn't fly). It grew and learned to fly and flew around our kitchen. It got so it would fly up into the window in the morning and peck to be let out. In the evening, it would again come back to the same window and peck to be let in for the night. This went on for some time, then one night, it didn't come back. We figured it had met some other flickers and decided to get married and live elsewhere!

That summer, I had my own construction site set up along the bank of the road in front of our barn. My brother's trucks and cars were being used for authenticity and there were tunnels and bridges built from dirt and clay. This equipment was quite safe left unattended during the night and all summer.

Chelley's hill had been flattened by now, and when you looked down the road, we could see Goldie's house. Hydro wires were going up between the poles and progress was everywhere! Our house was one of the first houses to be wired for electricity. We didn't need a lot of wiring, since we didn't have any electrical appliances. So, we got some ceiling lights

put in, which were quite a novelty. They consisted of a bare
bulb hung from a long wire and a pullchain for turning them
off and on. If Doris or I stood on our bed, we could reach the
pullchain—talk about being independent! We worked that
pullchain constantly when we got the chance! Anyone on the
outside of our house at night must have thought it was a honky
tonk, what with the flashing light in the window.

There was no talk of replacing the old hand-cranked
washing machine or purchasing a refrigerator. I would presume
there were also telephone lines, although we didn't get a
telephone. Kennedy's did, though, and once in a great while,
Dad would phone to let us know when we could expect him
home.

Lloyd Steves became our meter reader. He was a widower
with a daughter about my age and sometimes he'd bring her as
far as our house and leave her to play with us while he made
his rounds. I think my mother had a crush on him. He'd spend
some time visiting us (or maybe he was just concerned about
the safety of his daughter). Anyway, it was nice to have a
playmate my age, even if it was only for one day a month.

This was the summer a tornado/hurricane blew across the lake
quite unexpectedly and seemed to mainly hit our place and
Kennedy's. Our barn had been empty of hay for some time and
there was no floor in part of it. The barn was built about a foot
off the ground on pilings. Wind and hail came across the lake
and blew under the barn, lifted it up and set it down again—
only now it was partly hanging over the bank where my
construction site was. It didn't appear that it would tip over, so
for a while we had a barn that hung over that section of road.
Dad was home when this happened. He was right there in the
livingroom watching everything blow around. The hail was
beating the windows until I thought surely they'd break, or the
wind would blow them in. Dad was encouraging us kids to
come take a look at what was happening, so we pried ourselves
loose from Mom's grip under the diningroom table to join Dad
at the window. We had seen Kennedy's sow and the little

piglets take cover in the little pig house and suddenly the little house was lifted up and sailed away, around and around it went until it was out of sight. We learned later that it was set down again a half mile away and the pig and her babies were intact.

When everything settled down again, Dad and us kids went outside to check for damage. He checked the barn. I crawled under the barn to check my construction site. Then he checked around the house—no broken windows. However, our house had moved four inches off it's foundation. The barn was eventually moved back to where it had been, but I don't think anything was ever done about the house. Most of the leaves were missing from the trees in our yard and the lake was a muddy mess.

My mother always opened the outside cellar doors for the summer to ''air out the cellar.'' These doors were under the kitchen window and had a framework about ten inches wide on which the doors rested when closed. One day, Betty and I were playing on this framework, following each other up one side, across the top, and down the other side. There were concrete steps leading down to the concrete floor about eight feet below. Somehow, I managed to lose my balance at the top and went straight down the full eight feet to land on the top of my head on the floor below. Apparently I picked myself up, climbed the steps, walked over to the kitchen door, let myself in and collapsed on the kitchen floor. I don't recall doing this, and I honestly don't believe Betty pushed me. If anyone was to blame, it's you-know-who for allowing us to play such a dangerous game. Besides, we were doing it right under the kitchen window and you-know-who was in the kitchen!. About a week later when I regained consciousness, I was in a hospital, my head strapped down and flat on my back. The first thing I did was vomit. It was red and I knew it was blood.

Dad was sitting there in a chair by the window. He got the nurse to come and clean up the vomit, and he seemed so delighted to see me. It was still summer, but I thought I saw elves running by the window in a snowstorm and the windows

seemed to have bars on them. I tried to ask Dad about this, and
he laughed at me and said we were on the third floor of the
hospital. There were a lot of people around me, mainly in
white, and they were asking a lot of questions. Whether I
answered correctly or not didn't seem to matter. I think I was
out of it about seven days.

Dad was there pretty well every day. I presume Mom was
at home with the rest of the family. I couldn't recall exactly
what happened, except I did remember playing on the cellar
door frame. I don't know how long I stayed in the hospital, but
eventually I was allowed to get up and about. Dad brought me
some coloured macaroni and string, to make jewellery, and
paste and scissors and scrap books and read me stories. My
room was getting pretty full of activity projects and I know the
nurses were watching pretty closely at what I was doing.

The day eventually came that I was going home. Mom
came to my room and said Charlie was going to drive us home.
So we packed up all my pretty night gowns and toys and
"jewellery." All this stuff was new. Somehow Mom and I
were suddenly in a department store (or were we still in the
hospital?), and we were at the elevator door with my things
piled beside us when she left and told me not to move from
that spot. I didn't move and lost sight of her when, out of
nowhere, a woman dressed in all black walked up to me and
took all my things and never said a word—just walked away!
Mom was back almost immediately and asked about my things,
but when I told her a witch came and got them, she didn't
believe me. No one knows what really happened. I was having
a hard time making my brain work and give Mom the right
answers.

It was so good to be home. The dog was glad to see me and
Betty and Doris were curious about me. They didn't say
much—just stayed quiet. There was something in the house
that was making a dull roar and I asked Mom about it, but she
didn't know what I was talking about and I was told I would
get used to it—that it was okay and not to worry. Then the
house developed a whining noise and when I asked about it, I

was told it would eventually go away. The whine was louder outside and I decided it was being caused by the new hydro lines, since that was all that was reasonably new. I wasn't hearing voices, other than those I was supposed to hear, but I sure heard some weird sounds. At first they scared me, so I'd put my hands tight over my ears to try and drown out the sounds. They would seem to echo. I tried covering my head with a blanket to soften the sounds, but that didn't really help much. I couldn't seem to talk very well to Mom. She said I had an over-active imagination, but Betty and Doris were very good. If what I said didn't make much sense, they just went along with it and we went about our play (notice I said "play"— not fight).

School started again that fall and Doris was going to school too, but I was told I couldn't go for a while yet. That left just me and Walter at home with Mom and I soon got bored with that. One day I wanted to go down to the cellar and see the crack I'd supposedly made in the floor. Mom took me down, and while staring at it, she started to cry. I just stared at the star shaped crack and suddenly it took on the shape of a huge spider and I became hysterical, wanting out of there. I didn't venture down there for a long time. Apparently, I didn't tell Mom about the spider—I didn't want to be told I had an overactive imagination. Betty took up her teaching job at home and I seemed able to concentrate on what she was doing with me. My written work met with her approval, so I was let go back to school.

Betty was being very nice to me. We walked along and held hands and talked, but the kids at school were different. They took care of me. The teacher was very patient and gave me plenty of time to think before I was expected to answer. She allowed me to answer while seated, whereas the others were expected to stand to answer. I insisted on standing to answer, but soon found out this was not going to work too well. If I had to concentrate too hard, I'd faint. It was up to me if I wanted to remain seated or stand. I eventually decided not to talk around adults at all, since some of what I said caused the kids to cover their mouths and giggle. The teacher would try to make excuses for them. My written work was fine, so that was all that was expected of me. The silence around adults lasted for a long time. I needed to get my self-confidence back, it seemed, and I had to learn to distinguish between reality and imagination. I didn't mention the sounds I was hearing, but they too, seemed to be fading. I later learned I'd fractured my skull, causing a crack from the very top of my head, down the left side, all the way around to behind my left ear. Today, no sign of an injury will show up on an X-ray.

Walter was getting to be close to four years old by now. Mom still liked to leave his hair a bit long, so the curls remained. Poor little guy. He had to wear some of our hand-me-downs, and one winter his coat was pink. But he did have a proper boy's cap.

Joy's mother had by now been widowed and Joy had four younger siblings. Her mother acquired a car too, and she'd drive down to our house and bring the kids. One little girl was my age, Diane, and she too, went to the same school as did we!

By now Goldie was also going to the same school, but Goldie didn't go too much in the winter because of the distance and the cold.

Joy's mother had a sister in Boston, who would send parcels of used kids' clothing to her. She'd pick what she needed and the rest was brought to us. There was boy's clothing too, so Walter was getting to wear boy's clothes more often.

By now, Betty was responsible for all of us when we went out to play. Walter managed to topple out of the back of a rowboat that was tied to a tree, but the boat itself was in about two feet of water at the lake. We were all playing in the boat and suddenly, there he was, flat on his back under two feet of water. Betty pulled him up into the boat. He was coughing and crying, just like Doris did the day she fell off the pier. We stayed at the beach until Walter dried out, then set off home, promising each other that Mom must never know.

Doris hadn't adapted too well to keeping up with Betty and me and Walter seemed to be even slower. Doris never did learn to swim and we weren't about to take Walter on the pier.

One thing that Betty tried to pull off one day while eating wild raspberries and having Walter begging and pleading to have some too—he didn't want to go into the bushes, too prickly. We were sharing our raspberries with him until it got out of control. Betty managed to catch a dragonfly, or maybe it was already dead, and she broke the dragonfly into little pieces and stuffed a piece into each raspberry that she shoved into his mouth. Her fatal mistake came when she put the section with the wings still attached into a berry and he noticed it! He decided to cart it off home to show Mom what he was eating. What was the big fuss?—I'd eaten rabbit droppings all one summer! Even after this episode, Mom still insisted on sending him out with us.

We used him to test the safety of the lake ice in the late fall. We'd wait on the shore and tell him to hold onto the fence that went part way out into the lake. Sure enough, one day he broke through. He managed to hold on to the fence and work his way back to shore. His snowsuit was frozen stiff as we tried to walk him around to dry out, so we had to take him home and suffer the consequences.

Walter always had to be on our toboggan, too. He didn't like the dog biting his boots and he wouldn't take his turn pulling the toboggan up the hill. Because of all these hardships, he had to suffer, Mom eventually postponed sending him with us.

Our dog, Trixie, was a constant companion and this one was really quite smart. As well as being able to hunt snakes, it seemed he/she understood a fair bit of English.

The Kennedy's had chickens that were allowed to roam all over their own property, but none ever ventured down to our place unaided!. How this dog knew that "go fetch a chicken"

meant go tearing off up to Kennedy's, grab a chicken and
return, is a mystery. Maybe this Trixie was a natural retriever!
Us kids would go up to the barn, open the big front doors and
tell the dog, "Go fetch a chicken," (notice we would be safely
in the barn hidden from Mom's view!), and that ridiculous dog
would go tearing across the road at top speed and grab a
chicken, sometimes out of mid-air, and bring it to us. We
really didn't want a chicken, so we wouldn't take it from him
when it was dropped at our feet. Of course, the chicken would
try to fly and Trixie would jump into the air and bring it down
again and offer it to us. We would let this go on until we could
see the chicken was getting exhausted, but Trixie never tired of
trying to please us. Eventually, we'd take the chicken into the
barn, let it recuperate for a while and carry it back up to
Kennedy's. We did this a lot one summer, until Mom caught
the dog at it and the poor dog got a beating with a piece of
kindling wood. And then, she locked it in our own chicken/
playhouse. We didn't send the dog for any more chickens,
mainly because Mom said the next time us kids would get the
beating.

This Trixie loved to swim and would jump off the pier and
swim around with us. Then he/she too, would climb out on the
steps, drop in total exhaustion on the pier and catch a nap. Our
dogs never had pups that I can remember—only Scotty was
reproducing at this time. I think this Trixie got hit by a car and
died. We had a fair bit of traffic by now, but the road was still
gravel and dust.

You know, there is a point in everyone's life, whether they're
aware of it or not, that you try to make yourself more aware of
your surroundings, pay a little more attention to what's being
said and be a little more aware of the sounds and smells that
are all part of your environment.

Noticing the smell of the wet earth that spring we came
back to our farm from having lived on an island in the Atlantic
Ocean, was maybe the first time I had missed the smell of
something—like the smell of the ocean in the wind and the

different smell of the coal fire as compared to the smell of our wood burning stove; the gulls as compared to the crows; and the smell of the dusty road, compared to no smell at all on the island.

I'm now taking refuge in the long, sweet smelling hay. Just laying in there, inhaling the sweet smell of clover and dry hay, listening to the buzz of the bees working away on the clover heads. I can hear the water lapping at the shoreline. The crows are squawking away at each other and periodically, I see a small two-seater plane overhead, and it too, has a sound. I'm off in my dream world. Then Mom would call, "Supper," and disturb my world. Depending on how involved I was, would determine how quickly I got up and trekked off home.

The magpies were suddenly fascinating. They seemed to survive on cowpies in Kennedy's pasture. Beautiful black and white birds—always so rich in colour, as they pecked away at their meals. The cedar waxwings were always flitting about in the trees near the shoreline, wearing their little black masks. The humming birds would come to our honeysuckle bush and hang suspended in mid-air as they gathered their nectar. And the little sandpipers would run after a retreating wave and then race back up the beach, as the wave would roll in again. They never miscalculated the speed of the waves and they kept themselves from being washed away.

Kennedy's cows grazed silently in their pasture and the only way you could know they were even there, was by the tinkling of the bell attached to what appeared to be their leader. At dusk, they'd meander towards Kennedy's barn in anticipation of being milked. They were then returned to the pasture to spend the long warm nights. They knew to stay well away from the electric fence that was their enclosure.

The manure pile outside Kennedy's barn window would grow taller and taller until it was up to the windowsill, then it was loaded onto the wagon and hauled into the vegetable gardens or dumped onto Mrs. Kennedy's rose bushes. The manure pile was pleasantly scented with barn smells, and was so warm and squishy if you got into it with bare feet.

The big sow would grunt and use her nose to push her little piglets around. They'd give their little grunts and move on.

The lake was full of trails the clams would make as they went about their business, only to snap shut tightly if picked up and taken out of their familiar environment. The sunfish would travel about in schools and splash periodically as the whim struck them, or just for the sheer enjoyment of being alive in the fresh clean water.

We'd pick the wild asters and "butter and eggs" and make a bouquet for Mom, but according to her, they were full of bugs and the bottle of flowers would be put in the woodshed on the cover over the well.

Even though our apple trees had gone wild, the blossoms still smelled so sweet and the trees would produce small, scabby apples that smelled, well, of apples. Apples were our main fruit. The trees on the other farms were hardy and produced enough apples to feed everyone on the adjoining farms. Us kids were allowed to fry apples in butter and brown sugar for a treat and we had apple pies and apple betty. Mrs. Kennedy made the best—hers' had homemade butter and lots of cream and were always served warm in a cereal bowl.

All the farm women made their own bread, as did my mother. The crust on Mom's bread was always sharp, so we preferred to eat her bread soaked in warm milk and sprinkled with some sugar—it was called pap and it was our favourite cereal.

Beans and brown bread were always on the menu for Saturday nights, served up with lots of molasses and cornmeal bread—Johnny cake to us.

Another thing we seemed to eat a lot of was porridge. Mom would soak it overnight in a double boiler and try to make us eat it for breakfast. I could not swallow it—no way—it was just a slime ball to me. She would hide it in bread pudding and try to feed it to us at suppertime. One bite and we'd detect leftover porridge—no way. The poor dog would get it in his dish and would usually eat it, but not right away. He'd look pathetically at this blob in his dish, walk a few circles around it and look at

us as if he wanted it removed. Eventually, the dog would
approach the dish, circle it a few more times for courage and
gingerly curl his lips back out of the way and take a few small
bites with his front teeth. He'd do a few more circles and try
again until it was gone.

We were served parsnips. Fat chance of getting them into
me, but sure enough, they'd reappear in stew, end up on the
side of my plate and eventually, go into the dog dish. The dog
would perform the same ritual as with the porridge/bread
pudding.

Fishcakes: now they were okay, provided we had enough
catsup. They were a way of using up leftover, cooked
potatoes—all mashed in with canned chicken haddie and
chopped onions and made into small cakes the size of a
hamburger patty and fried in butter.

Scalloped potatoes were okay. Her corn scallop was okay,
too. She's use a can of creamed corn, mix it with milk and
flour and bake it until it was firm. All these things were made
with non-perishables, since we didn't have refrigeration.

When Dad was home, we'd have meat once in a while. The
neighbours would give us some deer meat on occasion and we
liked that. Mom would make mincemeat in canning jars for
pies.

She would, on occasion, "do down" some strawberries in
her canning jars and store these in the cellar on shelves. If us
kids happened to be playing in the cellar and got hungry, we
didn't hesitate to open a bottle of strawberries and scoop out a
mouthful. She always thought the fruit had shrunk when it
cooled. We would look at the jar, three-quarters full, and agree
with her.

We also caught fish with our homemade fishing poles. Dad
got us some real hooks and we used a willow or any thin
flexible branch, some string and the hook. Earthworms were
plentiful too. We would fish off the end of the pier. Dusk was
the best time. On occasion, we'd get an eel on our line, and
since we weren't about to touch it—they were known to wind
around our legs or wrists—the best way to get the eel off the

line, other than step on its tail and pull with all our strength, was to use the line with eel attached as a whip. This usually caused it to break loose and then we'd kick it along into the water again. It usually didn't swim too well after such a thrashing!

We didn't eat anything out of the lake that we caught. We usually threw everything back into the water. It was a bit tricky getting the sunfish off—they have very prickly fins. When Dad was home, he'd go fishing with us at dusk and make a great fire on the pier to attract the eels. And eels did come to his line, big ones. He didn't mind if they wound around his arm as he removed the hook from its mouth. Us kids would stand well back as this operation took place. I never witnessed Dad cooking these things, but I did witness him skinning them right there on the pier. He'd take out his whittling knife, make a cut around and just below their head and a short cut at the throat, grab onto the ''corner'' with his thumb and finger and rip the skin off, still in perfect condition—one long skin, just as if it had been shed. I think he may have cooked them up after everyone, including Mom, was in bed for the night. Mom couldn't stand seeing him eat these things and we weren't allowed to see it either.

On one occasion, Walter joined us on the pier to watch Dad catch his eels. He was in his ''training pants' only, when Dad pulled in a sunfish, took it off his hook, and dropped it into Walter's pants. The fish was flopping in there and Walter was screaming and doing some flips himself. Dad eventually got the fish out again and quieted Walter down, but it did leave some red scratches on Walter's belly which, of course, Mom noticed and Dad had to explain how that happened.

There was a little smokehouse on our property near the beach. I never saw it used for it's original purpose, but one time while going in there to warm myself, there was a mouse sitting there. I managed to corner and subdue it and to keep it warm, I put it in my pocket, but kept my hand in there, too. I walked around like that for some time. The little mouse stopped struggling after a while and remained relaxed. At day's end I removed it to see how it was and it was dead. I felt bad. Did I squeeze it too tight or did it just die from fright?

Dad had the greatest buoyancy of anyone I'd ever met. Of course, he was close to 250 pounds most of the time, but he could jump off the pier, feet first, and never get his head wet. I think I may have inherited some of this buoyancy, but certainly not all of it.

I thought I would experiment one day and instead of jumping with my legs closed, decided to jump spread-eagle. At first, when I hit the water, it was like I'd landed on a bowling ball and forced it up inside myself. I never thought I'd make it to the steps before I fainted, the pain was that great. No need to tell Mom, I just wouldn't do it again.

By now Walter was tagging along with us quite often. Both him and Doris had quiet personalities. Walter had blond hair, full of curls. Doris had beautiful platinum hair. Mine was dark brown and Betty's was honey blond. Us girls had straight hair and Mom kept Doris' hair cut short. But on occasion, Betty and I were allowed to let ours grow long enough to have braids. We didn't mind the braids, but Mom would pull them so tight, we always thought our eyes looked slanted. Sometimes, I would look in the mirror and would worry about my eyes never looking straight again.

My full lips worried me, too. And my eyebrows seemed to be growing together in the centre. I worried that I'd be called ''mono brow'' later in life. I also worried about the dark hair on my arms and legs and sometimes, when I was alone, I would borrow Mom's razor and shave my arms as well as my legs. Doris and Betty didn't have this problem.

Our car never got used that much anymore. The only friend Mom seemed to have was Joy's mother, ''Mrs. Bam,'' and since she had a car and wasn't afraid to drive, she'd bring all of her kids, including Diane, to our place for a visit in the summer. Us older kids would play in the lake. Joy and Betty would pair up and leave Diane and me on our own. Diane wasn't too good at swimming, so she and I would go off and do our own thing, maybe in the barn or maybe just along the beach exploring.

On occasion, Betty and I would go to their house which was about three miles away. They had chickens, a steer and an apple orchard. Of course, I was curious about the steer. It seemed to be always in a bad mood. Diane and I were told not to bother it, and we didn't. But I loved to sit on the cedar rail fence and watch it. If it came too close, I'd get down, but I think I caused Mrs. Bam some anxiety.

Diane and I were given the chore of feeding the chickens, usually. The Bamfords had barn cats and a phone. Mrs. Bam would make ice cream at times for us, but (sorry Diane), it always tasted like the barn and I wouldn't eat too much of it.

We'd have family picnics on their front lawn and enjoy the day. One morning when Joy ventured out into her own yard, she discovered a skunk had stuck it's head into a bottle and hadn't been able to get it out again. It was, therefore, trying to get away with the bottle interfering. Joy calmly and patiently approached the skunk from the front (country kids learn these things the hard way), and once she had the skunk calmed down, she proceeded to loosen the bottle. The skunk allowed her to do this, and once put back on the ground, seemed too weak to run off, so Joy got it some milk in the cat saucer. It lapped the milk and Joy refilled the saucer again and again. Joy was now petting it and talking softly to it. It seemed quite content to let her do this. This little skunk hung around their farm all summer and Joy tended to it with loving care. It became like a barn cat, and when not following Joy, it bedded down in the barn with the cats. The cats accepted it and she would find it curled up sleeping in the barn or outside sleeping in the sun. It eventually wandered off to join up with it's own kind.

Back at our own farm, the beautiful iridescent blue barn swallows were again building and rebuilding their nests of mud and grass under the overhang of our barn. They would soar around with grass hanging from their bills and locate their own nest, their long split tails trailing behind and their lovely orange breasts and black bills silhouetted in the sunshine. There were probably a hundred nests along the overhang and us kids would stand and just watch the activity for long periods of time. The nests were too high for us to peer into, but we knew what was happening in them.

The loons were always on the lake in early evening and early morning, calling to each other and echoing across the lake. We took it all for granted and assumed all people lived in this environment.

The bullfrogs would vie for their time too, in the evening, with their loud croaking, and on occasion, we'd listen hard and follow the sounds very quietly. If the frogs heard us approaching, they'd stop their croaking until they felt the danger had passed and would again start. We'd quietly sneak along in the tall grass, and many times, would find their hiding places and catch them for a thorough examination. On occasion, we'd find one with a limb missing from where the hay cutters had been too low to their hiding places.

We were entertained quite often by Doris when she was in the mood to entertain. She seemed to be double jointed and was tall and on the thin side, which was an asset when she'd demonstrate her chicken-laying-an-egg position (you may wish to try this at home): In a squat position, with her hands flat on the ground directly in front of her pelvis, she would lean slightly forward and put her weight on her hands and raise her feet up. Her butt would be clear of the ground and she'd swing her butt out behind as far as possible and then let gravity bring it down and forward. She'd swing like this until her arms got tired from her weight. With some encouragement from Betty and me, we could get her to be a little more adventuresome.

This, you may try at home, too, but only if it's comfortable! Butt on the ground, legs apart, take one leg and lift it up and place it behind your neck. Next, take the other leg and do the same thing. Once the legs are securely in place, put your hands on the ground directly in front of your pelvis, lean forward until your weight is all on your hands, lift your butt and swing back and forth quite freely. She would only last a short while doing this one, as her legs would get uncomfortable and she'd put her butt on the ground and ask Betty or myself to unhook her legs. She'd need some recuperation after this one, since her legs had been in an unnatural position and the blood needed to get back down to her feet. However, she never suffered any ill effects. I am afraid to think what would happen if Betty or I had wandered off and left her with her legs up behind her neck!

Some time around 1947, in mid-summer, we awoke to see our lake full of logs! The whole lake, as far as the eye could see, was LOGS. There was not a space left for swimming. Not a loon could be heard. Not a single lapping sound along the shoreline! Where ever did these come from? We wandered down to the pier and discovered there were two or three layers of logs, all around the pier. Later that day, we wandered up to the Horseshoe, and it too, was full of logs. The Kennedy boys came down to have a look and enjoy some fun. They got out onto the logs, fully dressed, and tried some log-rolling. They were good at it—they'd better be! If they were to lose their balance, they'd be under the logs with no way up. Us kids weren't ready to get into any competition with them just yet, so we observed and learned the art of log-rolling.

At first, we didn't jump from the pier onto a log. We would get on our logs from along the shore and then only in two or three feet of water in case we missed our footing. We wanted to be able to stand on the bottom of the lake if we "broke through."

This activity required some kind of footwear, as the logs had not yet been peeled and they were a bit slimy. We got to be pretty good at it—Betty and I more so than Doris. Doris' near drowning had made her a bit timid of the lake, but she'd walk along on the logs nearest the beach and be content to learn to keep her balance. Our knee-high rubber boots were the best protection for our feet and legs. Picture it, girls in shorts or homemade dresses and knee high rubber boots in mid-summer.

We left our boots on almost all the time now—the urge to log-roll came quite often. The Kennedy's explained what was happening and how the logs got there. It seems K.C. Irving was taking the logs that had been cut in the northern part of the province and floating them down the river into our lake on their way to his pulp mills in and around Saint John. Every few days we'd see strangers with peavy poles working along the shoreline, pushing the logs out into the lake again and again to keep them moving. They were very adept at walking on, and breaking up, any jammed logs and setting them free again. On occasion, a small tugboat would appear at our pier. This little tug was named *Purdy*, and it would be tied up at the end of our pier for days at a time while the longshoremen worked. We never met any of these men, as they were our enemy. We'd untie the *Purdy* and try to set it adrift, but it wouldn't move away because the logs had it blocked in.

On one occasion, Walter ventured down to the pier on his own and Mom discovered him laying on his belly with the top half of his torso hanging over the end of the pier between the pier and the *Purdy*. The lake was a bit rough that day and the *Purdy* was sloshing back and forth at the end of it's tether. Mom only ventured halfway down the pier and began calling him softly. He finally realized she was there and got up out of there without tumbling into the space between himself and the tug. Walter was born in 1942, so he wasn't quite five years old and I doubt he could swim. Even if he could, where was he going to swim to? The logs were there all that summer and were finally cleared from the lake shortly before freeze up.

Fall came and the leaves turned their usual red and gold before dropping to the ground and providing us with mounds of leaves to play in. We'd rake them into piles and then throw them around again, only to rake again and start over.

The hay would have been cut earlier by the Kennedy's, each with their own scythe. The sweet smells lasted for a few weeks before the stubble dried out and the scent was gone again for another year. We watched and participated in "getting in the hay'' with the Kennedy's. They'd have their pitchforks and big wooden rakes and make mounds of hay ready for the tractor to come along with a wagon on which to pitch the hay.

At times, Mr. Kennedy would pull me up onto the hay wagon and give me the job of stomping the hay down. One had to watch out for those flying pitchforks and not to step out too close to the edge of the wagon where the hay would hang over the sides. Betty and Doris would usually be on the wagon, too—did this man have patience! On occasion, we'd be allowed to steer the tractor from the lap of whoever was driving it. One time, when the full load of hay had been backed into their barn and placed directly under the ''block and tackle'' that was used to lift the hay from the wagon to the loft, I managed to get in the direct line of the hooks that were lowered to grab the hay. It hooked me by the dress, lifted me clear of the hay load and swung me up and into the loft! It was sort of fun when I realized it was done on purpose (I think!). Of course, I wanted to do it more often, but there was work to be done, so the boys got on with the job. Their barn smelled so good with the fresh hay and we were allowed to play there anytime we wanted.

We got some new neighbours by now. About two miles past our school, a family with four boys, all about our age, was going to operate a little country store that was down and off the main road about a quarter of a mile. Betty was in grade seven, I believe, and their oldest boy was in grade eight. Now, even though I was in grade six, I realized this guy was CUTE! Betty was smitten! She'd get the giggles and act coy around him. He'd tease her and she loved it. I just enjoyed watching them make total fools of themselves and maybe was a little jealous.

I used to wonder if he knew she wore heavy blue bloomers and had a blue-stained backside from getting wet with the snow!

The usual things were happening at home again that winter. The house was banked with fresh sawdust, the wood had been delivered and cut up—Mom doing most of it with some help with the splitting from us girls. It was always stacked neatly in the shed and it was always my job to tote it into the woodbox beside the stove in the kitchen.

We acquired a second cat from somewhere, which we named Pinky. Pinky wasn't as intelligent as Scotty. Scotty could let herself out and sometimes in as well. We didn't have an outside door on the front kitchen door and it took very little to turn the knob and the door would slowly open. Scotty would jump up with outstretched paws and turn the knob until the door slowly opened. It sometimes worked from the outside, but mainly, she'd just meow and we'd let her in. We had to close the door ourselves. After all, cats really don't care if the door is closed—it's more of a nuisance than a necessity.

So, getting back to Pinky. It was discovered that Pinky was using Betty's bedroom as a bathroom. Way back under the famous gold and white bed, lay a mound of dried-out cat droppings. Mom cleaned this up and washed it thoroughly with Creolin a few times, but it seemed Pinky was not going to go outside in the winter. One day, coming in from school and using the woodshed to get to the kitchen, there was my mother sitting on the wooden lard bucket with the lid on it. She'd been doing the laundry in the woodshed and had begun emptying the machine into the bucket, when Pinky must have came by on her way to Betty's bedroom (no doubt). Mom had Pinky in the bucket! The cat must have been putting up one heck of a struggle, because Mom was having a hard time keeping her balance, as she sat on the lid of the bucket. I may have been only a kid, but I knew this was no way to bath a cat!. So Pinky's life came to an end and I doubt anyone ever even remembered her name or her misfortune of not trying a little harder to give up her habit of using Betty's bedroom as a bathroom.

Christmas wasn't too exciting around our house. If we had dolls, Mom would make them some new clothes from scraps left from her attempts at making our dresses. She'd bake cookies and decorate them and sometimes we'd hang them on

the tree, but those decorations would disappear before
Christmas Day. We'd get Barley Toys (hard, coloured candy
shaped like animals), ribbon candy (pink and white striped,
hard candy in the shape of ribbon), chicken bones (chocolate-
filled, peppermint-flavoured, stick candy) and sometimes some
chocolates. These treats would come with the groceries from
Saint John.

One year, us kids discovered a big box of chocolates
hidden in a trunk in her room. By Christmas Day, there was
only the empty box. We all denied even knowing they'd been
there. I believe my brother was sick to his stomach a few times
just before Christmas. Mom was suspicious at that time, but
apparently, didn't check on the chocolates.

We had no electric lights for the tree, so we just hung balls
and strung some popcorn on it. If we were in need of a new
toboggan, we'd get that, maybe a sweater or two and some
cotton rib-knit stockings. We never believed in Santa anyway.
If Dad came home for Christmas, he'd sometimes bring a
bottle of wine. Mom didn't want him ''drinking'' so a fight
would break out. One year he gave Walter some wine and
Walter was sick the whole day. Us girls would get ourselves
into our heavy clothes and spend the day outside.

How do I speak about my mother and not be disrespectful?
You may have gathered by now that my affections lay with my
father and his with me.

My mother had glasses and dentures and in her rage at my
father or at us kids, she'd remove these articles and throw
them. Often the dentures, particularly, would get broken and
that would set her off into a hysterical screaming fit. Dad
would take us kids outside, as he could see no way to reason
with her. When he wasn't home, us kids would simply leave
the house until dark and sort of sneak in again at bedtime.

One comforting thing we noticed, was that both Betty and I
were almost as tall as she was by the time we were ten years
old. We could at least give her a menacing look eye to eye!

Although we never raised a hand to her or gave her any lip, we often wished we had a different mother. We'd feel bad about our feelings and try to be attentive to her expectations.

I know now that she probably suffered from deep depression, but back then, it was called mental illness. She never played with us, or read to us, or even ventured out of the house, unless company came by, which was rare. She would not associate with the neighbours and even Mrs. Bam's visits were few and far between.

To replace her dentures and glasses involved a trip to Sussex or Saint John. Although we still had the car, she really couldn't drive safely and never did get a license.

Her time was spent scrubbing the floors and applying paste wax. Us kids had to polish when she finished her part. The polishing was made into a game. We'd put some of the wool socks that Dad had been issued either on our hands or our feet and work away until we could slide with ease. She would strip wallpaper annually and redo the walls. She would wash ceilings and do a Morisco job on them.

Once, she actually took all the plaster off the living room and stripped the walls right down to the slats under the plaster. She redid it all to exactly as it had been before. She went through a lot of disinfectant and stovetop blackening and lye soap for the washing machine. Us kids would get scrubbed until I thought we'd bleed. She shingled the roof one summer and then proceeded to shingle the outhouse at the same time. And she did a perfect job.

One morning, when she was rearranging the kindling wood in the kitchen stove to keep the fire going, she stuck her hand into an open flame and her fuzzy sweater caught fire. It sort of went "poof" all over at once before she whipped it off and stomped on it. The fuzz was completely gone, as were her eyebrows and eyelashes and some of the front of her hair. Fortunately, she wasn't burned, but the sweater was ruined.

Another episode with fire occurred when Walter decided to become a full-time arsonist! He always seemed to have the

wooden kitchen matches in his pocket and laid threats on us
girls to set us on fire. He'd light little piles of leaves and grass
and fan these to keep them going. You could always find
Walter just by looking for his smoke signals. He built a raging
bonfire in our chicken/playhouse one day and when the
floorboards got burning and the smoke was really rolling—he
was in there with the door shut and the one window wouldn't
open—he got panicky and went to get Mom to help douse the
floorboards. He smelled pretty strong of smoke and was
coughing by this time, so Mom came running with the pail full
of water and got things under control again. We banned him
from the chicken/playhouse after that and threw all his little
treasures out into the yard. Mom eventually covered the floor
with linoleum, so it was ''clean'' again.

One bright sunny day, we had a knock on our door and there
stood a very handsome man in a full army uniform. Mom
seemed to know him, but the conversation went on at the front
door (she must have just scrubbed the floor). Eavesdropping,
as usual, us kids gathered he was another Kennedy just home
from his stint in the army. Talk was of selling our farmhouse.
    We knew Dad was now posted in Fredericton and seemed
to be home more often. This Kennedy son was named Lloyd
and he returned a few days later with a beautiful little red-
headed lady named Stella. Mom gave them a house tour. Us
kids were getting a bit scared about someone else living in our
house.
    Apparently, a deal was struck. We didn't pack up right
away, but we heard that Lloyd and Stella had married and were
looking forward to life on our farm!
    I believe the dealings with the sale of the house were being
worked out in either Sussex or Saint John, as Mom got us kids
ready for a ''business trip,'' one day that summer. On the way
to wherever in our car, she managed to hit the shoulder of the
gravel road and put the car over the bank. We rolled over about
three times before we came to a rest in a grassy field, upside
down. I had been in the backseat to start with and I remember

being on my back under the dash in the front when we came to a stop. All those wires.

A car that had been behind us came to a stop (he was still on the road). The driver came running into the field as we crawled out through the broken windshield. I remember him saying, "My God, Molly, are you trying to kill those kids?" Walter was yelling his head off, faking an injury, no doubt, but the rest of us were fine.

This man piled us into his car and we proceeded on our way. First we had to make a stop at the hospital to have Walter checked over. Nothing wrong—so he stopped yelling. Next, to a department store to replace Mom's torn stockings and then on to an office building where the man told Mom to go on by herself. He took us four kids for an ice cream, while we waited for Mom. After all this, he drove us home again.

Dad was called and told about the car. He wasn't too upset. In fact, I think he may have been relieved to know she wouldn't be driving it anymore. It must have gone to the junkyard, because it never did come back home.

Mom told us not to tell anyone we would be moving to Fredericton, but kids don't keep secrets like that! After all, we were going to live in a city where "we'd get a proper education!" I always thought we were getting a great education.

Betty was now in grade eight and there was no local high school, so it was sort of Betty's fault we had to move. Her newfound boyfriend took the news rather badly! He would grab her and kiss her turned-up little face every chance he got! The next oldest brother tried this on me. Ha! Fat chance I'd turn up my chubby little face for him!

So, as school neared an end that June, we started cleaning out our house. I was sad and I think my siblings were, too. We gave Trixie away, since "the city was no place for a dog" and Scotty was "done down" too, since she was old.

Furniture was being left behind for Lloyd and Stella to use. Dad came home to help with the move. He burned a lot of extras in a big bonfire on the beach. The butterfly collection was given to the school.

We watched silently. To my knowledge, no neighbours came by to say goodbye, but Dad made a few house calls with us kids in tow to say his goodbyes.

I was getting more upset by the minute and decided to make one more trip around to the Horseshoe by myself. I was sure going to miss all this, just so Betty could get an education!

It's now almost fifty years later. Lloyd and Stella still live in our old farmhouse and they raised six or seven children there. What marvellous stories that house could tell if only houses could talk.

About the Author

Jean (Young) Redekopp was born at home in a farmhouse on the shore of Grand Lake, New Brunswick in the late 1930s. In 1948 the Young family moved to Fredericton to join their father stationed at Point Ste. Anne.

After the culture shock of city life and high school, Jean married a local farm boy, produced a son, and worked for NB Telephone, Wandlyn Motels and the New Brunswick Government. In 1970, she moved to southern Ontario on her own, and in 1976 re-married and inherited a step-daughter.

Now widowed and retired, she enjoys a good life of travel, skiing, fishing, gardening, camping and canoeing.

Although she continues to live in a city, Jean prefers the country life and still refers to Grand Lake as ''home.'' She continues to enjoy the company of her sisters at their frequently get togethers.

Other Titles of Interest

Acorn, Milton. *Reading from **More Poems for People**.* 0-919957-62-5 (cassette) STE $9.95 *
Beutel (ed & cartoons). *True (Blue) Grit: A Frank McKenna Review in Cartoons and Essays.* 0-921411-53-7. MAPP $16.95 *
Blades, Joe. *Cover Makes a Set.* 0-919957-60-9. STE $8.95 *
Blades, Joe. *future now past.* 0-919957-61-7. STE $3.95
Blades, Joe, *Stones of My Flesh,* 0-919957-64-1. STE $2.95
Bull, Arthur; Bull, Ruth (ill.) *Hawthorn,* 0-921411-24-3. BJP $4.95
Deahl, James. *Under The Watchful Eye: Poetry and Discourse.* 0-921411-30-8 BJP $11.95 *
Deahl, James; *Under The Watchful Eye: Book and Video Set.* (incl. 0-921411-30-8, SF-93-501) 0-921411-31-6 BJP $34.95 *
Deahl, James; Fitzgerald, D.C. *Poetry and music from Under The Watchful Eye* (cassette) 0-921411-32-4, BJP $11.95 *
flaming, p.j. *voir dire.* 0-921411-26-X. New Muse 1994. BJP $11.95 *
Folsom, Eric. *Poems for Little Cataraqui.* 0-921411-28-6. BJP $10.95 *
Footman, Jennifer (ed) *An Invisible Accordion: A Canadian Poetry Association Anthology,* 0-921411-38-3, BJP $14.95 *
Footman, Jennifer *St Valentine's Day,* 0-921411-45-6, BJP $13.95 *
Gibbs, Robert. *Earth Aches,* 0-921411-36-7, BJP $2.95
Grace, Mary Elizabeth; Shin, Ann (eds). *Crossroads Cant: spoken word word as art song word.* 0-921411-48-0. BJP $13.95 *
Hawkes, Robert. *This Grievous Injury.* 0-921411-41-3. BJP $2.95
LeDuc, M.R., *Reflections of a Frog.* 0-921411-40-5. BJP $3.95
mclennan, rob *Poems from the Blue Horizon.* 0-921411-34-0. BJP $3.95
Pieroway, Charles Warren. *Sandy Point Map.* 0-921411-46-4. MAPP $4.95
Pieroway, Phyllis. *Memories of Sandy Point, St George's Bay, Newfoundland.* 0-921411-33-2. MAPP $14.95 *
Redekopp, Jean. *A View from the Bucket.* 0-921411-52-9. MAPP $14.95 *
Richards, David Adams. *A Lad from Brantford & other essays,* 0-921411-25-1. BJP $11.95 *
Schmidt, Tom. *The Best Lack All.* New Muse 1995. 0-921411-37-5. BJP $12.95 *
Smith, Diana. *Ripples from the Phoenix.* 0-921411-29-4. MAPP $2.95
Trakl, Georg; Skelton, Robin (translator) *Dark Seasons.* 0-921411-22-7. BJP $10.95 *
Vaughan, R.M. *The InCorrupt Tables.* 0-921411-44-8. BJP $2.95
Wendt, Karl. *Chaste Wood.* 0-921411-11-1. BJP $7.95 *

Ask your favourite bookstore to order these books (from General Distribution Services in Canada and the USA). Or order direct from us: individual orders must be prepaid and must include postage (in Canada: $2 for first * book + $1 each additional book, $0.75 per all other chapbook titles) and all Canadian orders must add 7% GST on the total books and postage (GST 12489 7943 RT****). All orders from individuals must be prepaid by cheque or money order. No credit card orders. No cash via post, please.

Order from:
M·A·P·PRODUCTIONS
BOX 596 STN A
FREDERICTON NB E3B 5A6
CANADA

Ph 506 454-5127
Fax 506 454-5127
E·mail jblades@nbnet.nb.ca